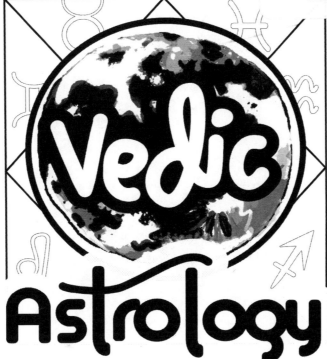

Vedic

Astrology

North Indian

CHART JOURNAL

108 Blank Chart Worksheets + Quick Guide

This Book Belongs to:

_____

Date:

_____

LUNAR
PERSUASION

ISBN: 978-1-965691-02-1

Dedicated to Taz, Z and Noah

A special thank you to Svati Singh for her proofreading assistance.

Written and designed by Christina Linard

1st edition 2024

www.lunarpersuasion.com

Contents

i.   How to Use This Book

ii. Sample Page

iii. Signs, Elements, Modes

iv. The 9 Planets or Grahas

v.   The 12 Houses

vi. House Type and Karaka

vii. The 3 Gunas,
     Combustion,
     Conjunction, Dasha

viii. Dignity, Directional
      Strength, Gandanta,
      Hemming, Karaka, Lord,
      Masculine and Feminine

ix. Nakshatras Opposition,
     Planetary Aspect

x.   Retrograde, Sidereal
     Zodiac, Stationary,
     Tropical Zodiac, Yoga

How to Use This Book

This book is a companion tool for anyone wanting to study Vedic Astrology and learn how to read the significations shown in a chart quickly. Vedic Astrology is a vast subject with many layers of depth and analysis that are outside the scope of this book. However, the reference pages provide some keywords and concepts to get started and inspire your astrological interpretations.

Begin a chart analysis with a blank worksheet. Write in the birth details, including name, date, time, and location of the person or event. Write the planet's initials or glyph in each house of the blank chart, along with its degrees and minutes. You may obtain this astrological information with an online chart calculator or Vedic Astrology software.

Below the chart, you'll find a table where you can write in the planets as house rulers, their karakas and significations, sign and dignity. As you fill in the details, take a moment to note each combination and position. The reference pages are there to guide you, providing a sense of inspiration and support as you write down your thoughts and interpretations.

Use the section next to the chart to fill in the Dasha years, events that occurred, or for oppositions and conjunctions of each planet. Once all information is in front of you, it's time to put your observations to work. Look for a confluence of themes, elements, and areas of life that could be challenging or auspicious. Is there a masculine planet in a feminine sign? Is there a Dharmic planet in a Tamasic sign? Are there planets in aspect with the same or close degree? Does the planet's energy work well with the significations of the houses they rule, or is there a malefic aspect creating challenges on a benefic planet or house? These are just some questions you can ask when writing down the details and documenting your observations. Your insights are key to the interpretation process.

Use the worksheets to demystify charts or draw up the New Moon transit and analyze the houses impacted for each Ascendant.

Date _____   Time _____   Location _____   Name _____

	ASC
	KETU
	VENUS
	SUN
	MOON
	MARS
	RAHU
	JUPITER
	SATURN
	MERCURY

DASHA CYCLES MILESTONES EVENTS ASPECTS YOGAS ETC.

SUN	MOON	MARS	MERCURY	JUPITER	VENUS	SATURN

GET CREATIVE IN THIS SPACE THAT'S ALL ABOUT THE PLANETS

Planet ————— Sign

HOUSE	LORD	RC	in HOUSE/SIGN	KARAKA	DIGNITY	GUNA	SEX	MODE	ELEMENT	AIM
1 SELF										
2 VALUES										
3 EFFORT										
4 HOME										
5 CREATE										
6 HEALTH										
7 PARTNER										
8 CHANGE										
9 DHARMA										
10 ACTION										
11 FRIENDS										
12 EXPENSES										
RAHU / KETU										

LOOK AT PLANETS AS HOUSE LORDS OR READ AS ASCENDANTS FOR THE CURRENT TRANSITS.

USE THE LIGHT GRID TO DRAW IN EXTRA CHARTS OR CUSTOM COLUMN HEADERS

The 12 Zodiac Signs or Rashis A 360 degree belt of stars that rise and set on the horizon. The sign gives personality and character to its house and to any planets in the house.

♈ Aries: Rajas, Fire, Movable, Masculine, Mars ruled

♉ Taurus: Rajas, Earth, Fixed, Feminine, Venus ruled

♊ Gemini: Rajas, Air, Dual, Masculine, Mercury ruled

♋ Cancer: Sattwa, Water, Movable, Feminine, Moon ruled

♌ Leo: Sattwa, Fire, Fixed, Masculine, Sun ruled

♍ Virgo: Tamas, Earth, Dual, Feminine, Mercury ruled

♎ Libra: Rajas, Air, Movable, Masculine, Venus ruled

♏ Scorpio: Tamas, Water, Fixed, Feminine, Mars ruled

♐ Sagittarius: Sattwa, Fire, Dual, Masculine, Jupiter ruled

♑ Capricorn: Tamas, Earth, Movable, Feminine, Saturn ruled

♒ Aquarius: Tamas, Air, Fixed, Masculine, Saturn ruled

♓ Pisces: Sattwa, Water, Dual, Feminine, Jupiter ruled

Modality of a Sign

Movable: Aries, Cancer, Libra, Capricorn, initiators, leaders, dynamic, proactive, starting new projects, ambition, drive, original Movable houses are 1, 4, 7, and 10

Fixed: Taurus, Leo, Scorpio, Aquarius, stable, determined, reliable, persistent, seeing through to completion, resistance to change, original fixed houses are 2, 5, 8, 11

Dual: Gemini, Virgo, Sagittarius, Pisces, adaptable, flexible, ability to bring things to a conclusion and prepare for new beginnings, original Dual houses are 3, 6, 9, 12

The Sign's Elements

Fire Aries, Leo, Sagittarius, Sun, Mars, transformation, energy, vigor, strength, action, courage, initiative, individual, purification, inspiration, original houses 1, 5, and 9

Earth Taurus, Virgo, Capricorn, Mercury stability, solids, smell, odor, support, grounded, security, practical, cautious, original houses 2, 6, and 10

Air Gemini, Libra, Aquarius, Saturn, light touch, communication, ideas, achievement, wealth, social, intellect, original houses 3, 7, 11

Water Cancer, Scorpio, Pisces, Venus, Moon, wavering movement, intuitive, emotions, flow, nurturing, receptive, original houses 4, 8, 12

The 9 Planets or Grahas

Sun: soul, self-realization, purification, vitality, father, honor, cruel, malefic, sattwa, masculine, rules Leo, exalted in Aries, debilitated in Libra, active energy, Atmakaraka, rules Sunday, Friends–Jupiter, Mars, Moon, Enemies– Saturn, Venus, Mercury, Digbala – South

Moon: emotional mind, mother, happiness, impressionable, travel, face, fame, moving, sleep, benefic, sattwa, feminine, rules Cancer, exalted in Taurus, debilitated in Scorpio, receptive energy, the lens through which we experience everything in life, rules Monday, Friends with all, Digbala– North

Mars: courage, action, willpower, anger, strength, change, brother, malefic, tamas, masculine, rules Aries and Scorpio, exalted in Capricorn, debilitated in Cancer, disruptive transformation, catalyst for action and change, rules Tuesday, Friends– Sun, Moon, Jupiter, Enemies– Saturn, Venus, Mercury, Digbala – South

Mercury: education, communication, intelligence, business, health, interests, writing, talking, social media, witty, quick, rajas, neutral, rules Gemini and Virgo, exalted in Virgo, debilitated in Pisces, the thinking mind, dedicated to neutrally delivering the message, rules Wednesday, Friends– Venus, Saturn, Enemies– Sun, Mars, Jupiter, Digbala– East

Jupiter: knowledge, wisdom, teacher, children, religious perception, abundance, expansion, big, philosophy, luck, benefic, sattwa, masculine, rules Sagittarius and Pisces, exalted in Cancer, debilitated in Capricorn, our inner guidepost, happiness in our beliefs and outlook on life, rules Thursday, Friends– Sun, Moon, Mars, Enemies– Saturn, Venus, Mercury, Digbala– East

Venus: beauty, desire, marriage, relationships, our values, compromise, agreements, money, wealth, women, sensual pleasures, jewelry, art, cars, fashion, benefic, rajas, feminine, rules Taurus and Libra, exalted in Pisces, debilitated in Virgo, how we feel valued in relationships, rules Friday, Friends– Saturn, Mercury, Enemies– Sun, Mars, Jupiter, Digbala– North

Saturn: longevity, profession, responsibility, karma, adversity, time, restriction, delay, pressure, old age, cold, malefic, tamas, neutral, rules Capricorn and Aquarius, exalted in Libra, debilitated in Aries, represents time and a pressuring influence on what is not correct or true dharma, rules Saturday, Friends– Venus, Mercury, Enemies–Mars, Jupiter, Sun, Moon, Digbala– West

Rahu: power, confusion, illusion, holding on, insatiable desires, hunger, inexperience, the head of the dragon with no tail, North Node of the Moon, shadow planet and co-rules Aquarius, always 180° from Ketu, retrograde movement

Ketu: perfectionism, spirituality, letting go of past life achievements, the tail of the dragon with no head, co-ruler of Scorpio, always 180° from Rahu, South Node of the Moon, a shadow planet, retrograde movement

The 12 Houses of a chart represent the different areas of life where karma is created and experienced. Each house contains a full sign. Houses take on the influence of the planets they hold as well as the nature of the sign in the house. Houses also take on the qualities of any special aspects and oppositions. A house without a planet is capable of being the strongest or weakest house depending on the aspects and placement of its ruler in the chart.

First House: Ascendant/Lagna, individuality, appearance, physical body, overall health, self, dharma house, kendra house, trinal house, associated with Aries, Sun, Jupiter and Mercury gain directional strength, Eastern horizon, and sunrise

Second House: wealth, money, family, speech, communication, food, face, values, precious metals and stones, artha house, associated with Taurus

Third House: self-effort, interests, performing arts, social media, journeys, siblings, courage, hands, desires, kama house, associated with Gemini

Fourth House: home, mother, comfort, land, treasures, connecting to the heart, moksha house, kendra house, associated with Cancer and the Moon, North direction, and midnight

Fifth House: creativity, intellect, children, romance, mantras, heart's desire, dharma house, trinal house, associated with Leo and Jupiter

Sixth House: health, service, disease, injury, enemies, co-workers, hard work and sacrifice, daily tasks, artha house, dusthana house, associated with Virgo

Seventh House: partnership, spouse, marriage, contracts, trade, business, desires, kama house, kendra house, associated with Libra, Saturn has directional strength here, Western horizon where Sun sets

Eighth House: transformation, inheritance, longevity, occult matters, fear, battles, scandals, moksha house, dusthana house, associated with Scorpio

Ninth House: philosophy, distant travel, religion, father, higher learning, law, luck, dharma house, trinal house, associated with Sagittarius

Tenth House: karma, career, reputation, authority, public life, artha house, kendra house, associated with Capricorn. Sun, Mars, and Saturn gains directional strength, South direction, high noon

Eleventh House: gains, friendships, achievements, aspirations, older siblings, large organizations, artha house, kama house, associated with Aquarius

Twelfth House: loss, isolation, confusion, expenses, spirituality, bed pleasures, surrender, hospitals, moksha house, associated with Pisces, dusthana house

House Types define the different groupings of houses that tell a bigger picture from the individual house meanings. Houses 1-4 are about self development, houses 5-8 are about development with others and houses 9-12 are about the development of something bigger than ourselves and others.

Dharma Houses: truth about life's purpose.
1st House: self and identity
5th House: creativity and children
9th House: higher learning and religion

Artha Houses: wealth, health and work
2nd House: finances and possessions
6th House: work and health
10th House: career and social status

Kama Houses: desires, relationships, goals
3rd House: communication and siblings
7th House: partnerships and marriage
11th House: friendships and aspirations

Moksha Houses: deep transformation, spirituality, surrender
4th House: home and emotional security
8th House: transformation and secrets
12th House: solitude and spiritual enlightenment

Upachaya Houses: planets here will improve over time
3rd House: self-effort and willpower
6th House: enemies and health
10th House: karma and duty
11th House: achievements and goals

Dusthana Houses: challenges and obstacles
6th House: health, enemies, and obstacles, service to others, and self-improvement
8th House: transformation, secrets, longevity, death, and rebirth
12th House: losses, expenses, spiritual liberation, isolation, confusion, foreign lands, and the subconscious

Kendra Houses: the four pillars of life
1st House: self, physical body, overall health
4th House: home, family, peace of mind
7th House: partnerships, spouse, relationships
10th House: career, status, karma, public life

Trinal Houses: bring luck, prosperity, ease
1st house: self, similar to its role as a Kendra
5th House: creativity, children, education
9th house: higher learning, spirituality, the most auspicious house in the chart

House Karakas

1st: Self	7th: Spouse
2nd: Wealth	8th: Life Span
3rd: Willpower	9th: Religion
4th: Connections	10th: Career
5th: Creativity	11th: Gains
6th: Health	12th: Expenses

The 3 Gunas: Sattwa, Rajas, and Tamas are the three major qualities of intellect that define the tendencies within all of us. A person will have a balance or imbalance of these three qualities, as seen in the chart, through the signs and planets in houses.

Tamas is the inactive and unknowing part of our intellect where darkness prevails, and the lack of light is a lack of consciousness; in Tamas, Fire, Water, Earth, Air, and Ether manifest. Mars and Saturn are Tamasic planets.

Rajas is where we actively fulfill desires and perform actions. The need to consume outweighs any other desire. This quality is where the five elements are experienced through our senses: hearing, sight, smell, taste, and touch.

Sattwa is our intelligence and higher-thinking mind—a pure and true nature that has the power to control and liberate us from Rajas and Tamas. The Sun, Moon, and Jupiter are all Sattwic planets.

Combustion occurs when a planet is very close to the Sun. This proximity to the hot, burning luminary can diminish the planet's natural qualities and create frustration and agitation because it cannot perform at full capacity. The example in Chart A shows every planet within its orb of combustion. Mercury is combust when it is within 14° of the Sun on either side. The Moon is combust at 12° or less. Mars is 12° or less, Jupiter is 11° or less, Venus is 10° or less, and Saturn is combust 16° or less from the Sun. Planets within their orb of combustion, but in another sign or house, are still considered to be combust.

Conjunction occurs when planets are in the same house. They continuously affect each other with their benefic or malefic nature. In chart A, Mars, Mercury, Saturn, and Moon are all in conjunction in the 4th House of Taurus.

Dasha or Mahadasha is a major cycle of time ruled by a specific planet. The position of your natal Moon and nakshatra determines the dasha cycle you begin with at birth. As you live life, you experience the different dasha cycles along the way. The dasha system is a powerful tool for making predictions and is used alongside the current transit chart to analyze how they interact with the natal planets. Each dasha cycle has a specific duration depending on the planetary ruler and always follows the same planetary order, starting with Ketu, then Venus, Sun, Moon, Mars, Rahu, Jupiter, Saturn and Mercury. A dasha has a major (maha) cycle and a sub-cycle, Antar dasha, using the same planetary order. Each Mahadasha cycle is listed below in terms of years.

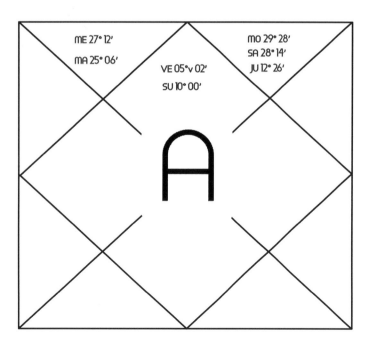

ME 27° 12'
MA 25° 06'

VE 05° v 02'
SU 10° 00'

MO 29° 28'
SA 28° 14'
JU 12° 26'

A

Ketu 7
Venus 20
Sun 6
Moon 10
Mars 7
Rahu 18
Jupiter 16
Saturn 19
Mercury 17

Dignity of a planet is determined by the sign and house a planet is in. Planets in their own or exalted sign will produce results relative to their nature with greater ease than if they were in a debilitated sign.

Digbala mens directional strength and is gained when a planet is in a specific direction or house. The planet's natural qualities are supported in that environment and operate at full strength, assuming there is no other aspect to consider. The opposing house shows where the planet has no Digbala.

North/4th House: Venus and Moon

East/1st House: Mercury and Jupiter

South/10th House: Suna and Mars

West/7th House: Saturn

Gandanta is a portion of the zodiac symbolizing a karmic knot and only occurs when a planet is in the final 48 minutes of a water sign or the first 48 minutes of a fire sign. Gandanta appears three times across the span of the zodiac. Challenges and obstacles impact planets when they are within a gandanta point. The native will experience extreme karma in the areas of life indicated by the houses.

Hemming occurs when a planet is between two malefic or two benefic planets. The malefic planets bring challenges and obstacles, while the benefic planets support the planet being hemmed.

Karaka means indicator. Each planet is a karaka for some aspect of our life. All that exists can be associated with a planet by its karaka. (Refer to Grahas on page iv)

Lord is a planetary ruler of a house based on which sign is in that house. Mars will rule the second house if Aries or Scorpio are there, while Jupiter could be the second house lord if Sagittarius or Pisces are there. If, in the chart, the Sun is in Gemini, then Mercury, as ruler of Gemini, will also rule the Sun. Therefore, the Sun will take on the qualities of its house lord, Mercury.

Masculine and Feminine are the push and pull of the Universe. Masculine energy is active, action-oriented, and has a positive charge. Feminine energy is inactive, receptive, and has a negative charge. Neutral signs do not carry a charge.

Sun represents pure masculine energy and gives without receiving. This is observed everyday when the Sun rises and brings its warming rays to life on Earth. The Moon is purely receptive and its light is only a reflection of the light that the Sun gives.

The Sun and Moon each rule one sign., Leo and Cancer respectively. The planets, however, rule two signs each, a feminine and a masculine sign, showing their dual nature.

Nakshatras are fixed stars nestled within the 360° sidereal zodiac. There are 27 Nakshatras, each forming a special relationship with the Moon. As the Moon and the other planets travel simultaneously through the signs and nakshatras, the effects will vary depending on how much they like to be in that space. Nakshatras have a planetary ruler that activates them during the mahadasha or antar dasha cycle of that planet.

1. Ashwini (Ketu)
2. Bharani (Venus)
3. Krittika (Sun)
4. Rohini (Moon)
5. Mrigishira (Mars)
6. Ardra (Rahu)
7. Punarvasu (Jupiter)
8. Pushya (Saturn)
9. Aslesha (Mercury)
10. Magha (Ketu)
11. Purva Phalguni (Venus)
12. Uttara Phalguni (Sun)
13. Hasta (Moon)
14. Chitra (Mars)
15. Swati (Rahu)
16. Vishaka (Jupiter)
17. Anuradha (Saturn)
18. Jyestha (Mercury)
19. Mula (Ketu)
20. Uttara Ashadha (Venus)
21. Purva Ashadha (Sun)
22. Shravana (Moon)
23. Dhanistha (Mars)
24. Shatabishak (Rahu)
25. Purva Bhadrapada (Jupiter)
26. Uttara Bhadrapada (Saturn)
27. Revati (Mercury)

Opposition occurs when a planet is seven signs away from another planet. Oppositions create power and influence between the planets. During transits, oppositions to natal planets can bring major changes and disruptions, especially if the native has not followed their dharma.

Planetary aspect occurs when a planet is "looking" at another planet/sign/house and throws its influence as a karaka/house ruler onto the other planet and house. Some aspects have unique names, such as the opposition or the conjunction. Each planet will throw its effect, relative to its nature, onto the house and planet in sight.

The slower-moving planets have special aspects seen in both the natal chart and by transit. **Jupiter aspects 5th and 9th from itself, Mars– 4th and 8th , Saturn– 3rd and 10th.**

It is important to remember that when counting houses, always start with the house that is throwing the aspect as one, the next house as two and so on. Chart **B** shows an example of how the planets can aspect each other. Mars aspects Venus and Mercury. Saturn aspects the Sun and the Ascendant. Jupiter aspects the Moon and the Ascendant.

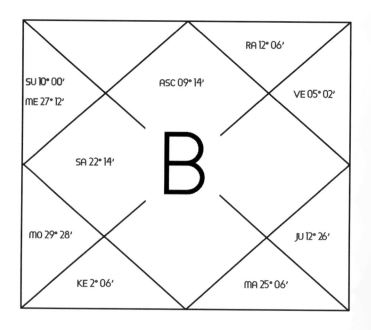

Retrograde planets appear to move backward as their orbit brings them closer to Earth. Natives with a retrograde planet tend to be more introspective, while their karmic fruits come later in life. By transit, a retrograde planet revisits the actions of our most recent past relative to what the planet deals with and which house is involved.

- Mercury slows down to retrograde three times a year for approximately three weeks at a time.

- The Sun and Moon never retrograde.

- Venus retrogrades about every 18 months for approximately 40 days.

- Mars retrogrades for two months, about every two years.

- Jupiter and Saturn retrograde about 5 months of a year

Sidereal Zodiac is a 360° cosmic belt comprised of the twelve signs and are aligned with the 27 fixed nakshatras.

Stationary is a term used to describe the speed and movement of the planet before it turns retrograde or direct. The planet slows down and holds the same degree for a few days, then stops before changing direction. The stationary degree of a transiting planet is powerful when it aligns with a natal planet of the same degree or a few degrees on either side.

Tropical Zodiac, also comprised of the twelve zodiac signs, is in alignment with the four seasonal equinoxes of Earth: Spring, Summer, Autumn, and Winter. The precession of the Earth's oval-shaped rotation, gradually shifts the timing of the tropical zodiac to no longer align with the fixed stars.

Yoga is a combination of planets as house rulers in certain aspects with each other. Hundreds of yogas are possible in a chart, and it may be impossible to remember them all. Luckily, some common Yogas are easy to identify with little practice. Yogas give a special effect or outcome that can be observed and applied to other factors in the chart. They are also used to make accurate predictions and conclusions about the native's karma. Yogas can be auspicious or inauspicious and are fully activated when that planet's dasha or antar dasha cycle runs.

Mahaparusha Yoga occurs when a Planet is in its own sign or is in a sign where it is exalted and in a Kendra house. This yoga gives a "kingly" effect relative to that planet as a karaka and house ruler.

Dhana Yoga is a wealth-producing yoga that occurs when the 1st, 2nd, 5th, 9th, and 11th house lords form a combination

Raj Yoga is auspicious, bring luck and occurs when the lord of a Kendra house interacts with the lord of a trine house, such as the fifth lord in the 10th house, for example.

Parivartana Yoga is when two lords are in each others house like Jupiter in Capricorn, while Saturn is in Pisces. This energy exchange can be supportive or divisive, depending on the nature of the planets involved, but overall is a strong influence.

Extended Study

Vedic Astrology is a lifetime of study. Here are some books and other resources that have helped me along the way.

The Vedic Astrology software I use is **Parasharas Light v9**. There are also free chart generators available online.

An extensive database of documented biographies with accurate birth times is available on **www.astro.com**.

Brihat Parasara Hora Sastra: A Compendium in Vedic Astrology Vol. 1 & 2 by Girish Chand Sharma.

Light on Life: An Introduction to the Astrology of India by Hart de Fouw and Robert Svoboda

The Nakshatras: The Lunar Mansions of Vedic Astrology by Komilla Sutton

The Ascendant: 108 Planets of Vedic Astrology by Sam Geppi.

Ancient Hindu Astrology for the Modern Western Astrologer; The Braha Sutras: Insights from a Lifetime of Vedic Astrology by James Braha.

Astrology of the Seers: A Guide to Vedic/Hindu Astrology by David Frawley

Visit www.lunarpersuasion.com to download my free e-book:
How to Read a South Indian Style Chart

For Natal Chart readings, email info@lunarpersuasion.com.

Date   Time   Location   Name

ASC

| KETU |
| VENUS |
| SUN |
| MOON |
| MARS |
| RAHU |
| JUPITER |
| SATURN |
| MERCURY |

| SUN | MOON | MARS | MERCURY | JUPITER | VENUS | SATURN |

Planet —————————————————————————— Sign

HOUSE	LORD	RC	in HOUSE/SIGN		KARAKA		DIGNITY	GUNA	SEX	MODE	ELEMENT	AIM
1 SELF												
2 VALUES												
3 EFFORT												
4 HOME												
5 CREATE												
6 HEALTH												
7 PARTNER												
8 CHANGE												
9 DHARMA												
10 ACTION												
11 FRIENDS												
12 EXPENSES												
RAHU / KETU												

Date	Time	Location	Name

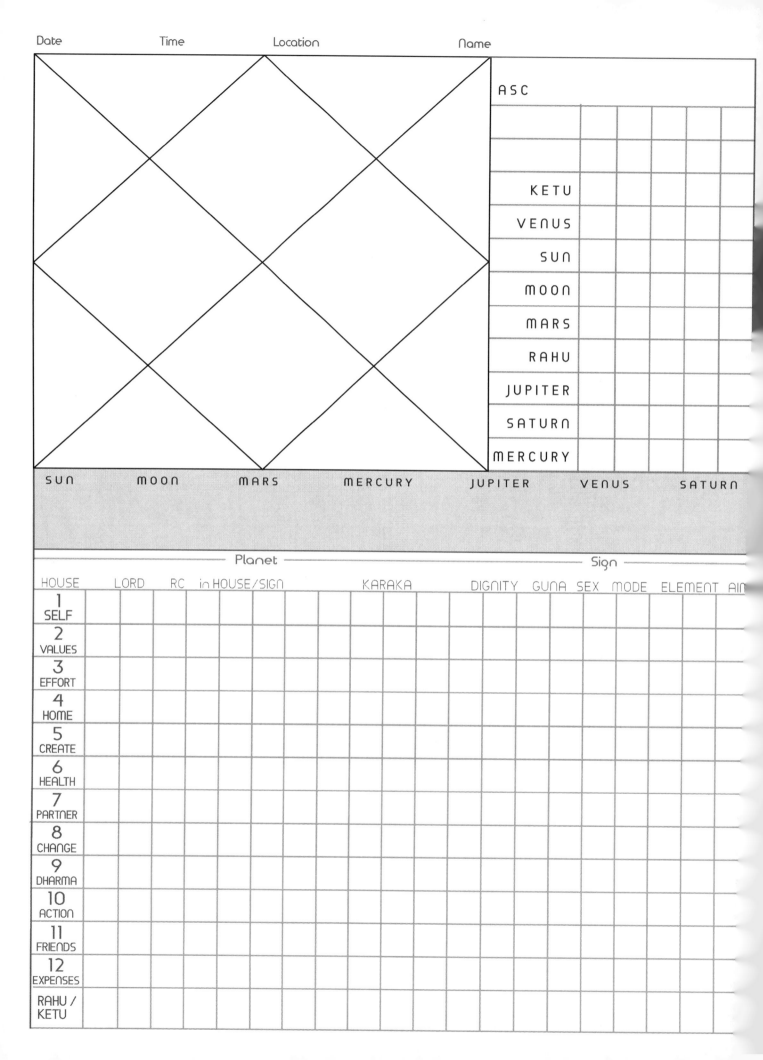

ASC

KETU
VENUS
SUN
MOON
MARS
RAHU
JUPITER
SATURN
MERCURY

SUN   MOON   MARS   MERCURY   JUPITER   VENUS   SATURN

——— Planet ———   ——— Sign ———

HOUSE	LORD	RC	in HOUSE/SIGN	KARAKA	DIGNITY	GUNA	SEX	MODE	ELEMENT	AIM
1 SELF										
2 VALUES										
3 EFFORT										
4 HOME										
5 CREATE										
6 HEALTH										
7 PARTNER										
8 CHANGE										
9 DHARMA										
10 ACTION										
11 FRIENDS										
12 EXPENSES										
RAHU / KETU										

Date	Time	Location	Name

ASC

KETU					
VENUS					
SUN					
MOON					
MARS					
RAHU					
JUPITER					
SATURN					
MERCURY					

SUN	MOON	MARS	MERCURY	JUPITER	VENUS	SATURN

—————— Planet ——————   —————— Sign ——————

HOUSE	LORD	RC	in HOUSE/SIGN	KARAKA	DIGNITY	GUNA	SEX	MODE	ELEMENT	AIM
1 SELF										
2 VALUES										
3 EFFORT										
4 HOME										
5 CREATE										
6 HEALTH										
7 PARTNER										
8 CHANGE										
9 DHARMA										
10 ACTION										
11 FRIENDS										
12 EXPENSES										
RAHU / KETU										

Date	Time	Location	Name

ASC

KETU					
VENUS					
SUN					
MOON					
MARS					
RAHU					
JUPITER					
SATURN					
MERCURY					

SUN	MOON	MARS	MERCURY	JUPITER	VENUS	SATURN

Planet — **Sign**

HOUSE	LORD	RC	in HOUSE/SIGN			KARAKA		DIGNITY	GUNA	SEX	MODE	ELEMENT	AIR
1 SELF													
2 VALUES													
3 EFFORT													
4 HOME													
5 CREATE													
6 HEALTH													
7 PARTNER													
8 CHANGE													
9 DHARMA													
10 ACTION													
11 FRIENDS													
12 EXPENSES													
RAHU / KETU													

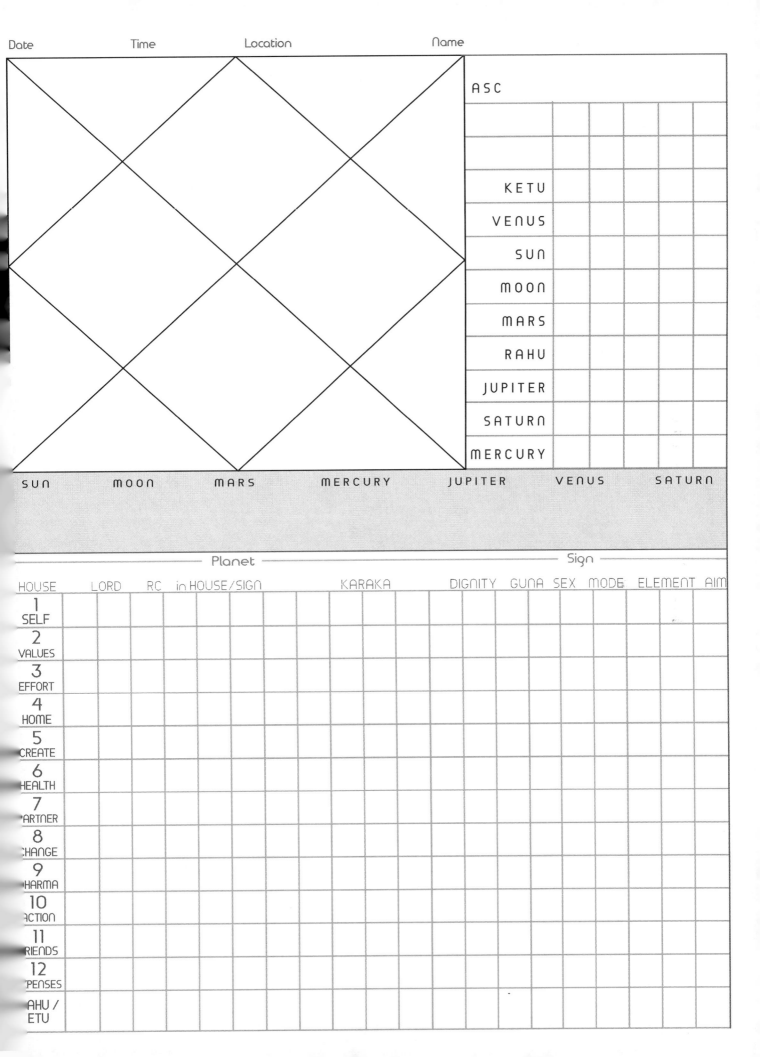

Date   Time   Location   Name

ASC

KETU					
VENUS					
SUN					
MOON					
MARS					
RAHU					
JUPITER					
SATURN					
MERCURY					

SUN   MOON   MARS   MERCURY   JUPITER   VENUS   SATURN

――――― Planet ―――――   ――――― Sign ―――――

HOUSE	LORD	RC	in HOUSE/SIGN			KARAKA		DIGNITY	GUNA	SEX	MODE	ELEMENT	AIM
1 SELF													
2 VALUES													
3 EFFORT													
4 HOME													
5 CREATE													
6 HEALTH													
7 PARTNER													
8 CHANGE													
9 DHARMA													
10 ACTION													
11 FRIENDS													
12 EXPENSES													
RAHU / KETU													

Date	Time	Location	Name

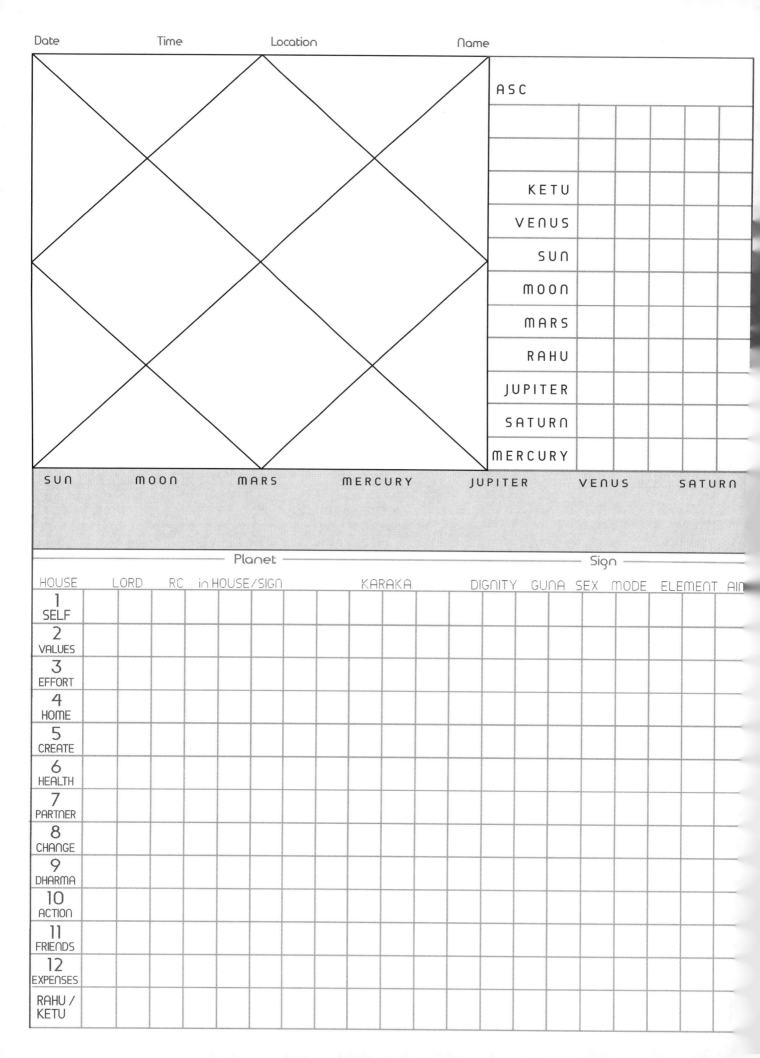

ASC

| KETU |
| VENUS |
| SUN |
| MOON |
| MARS |
| RAHU |
| JUPITER |
| SATURN |
| MERCURY |

SUN	MOON	MARS	MERCURY	JUPITER	VENUS	SATURN

Planet							Sign					
HOUSE	LORD	RC	in HOUSE/SIGN			KARAKA	DIGNITY	GUNA	SEX	MODE	ELEMENT	AIM
1 SELF												
2 VALUES												
3 EFFORT												
4 HOME												
5 CREATE												
6 HEALTH												
7 PARTNER												
8 CHANGE												
9 DHARMA												
10 ACTION												
11 FRIENDS												
12 EXPENSES												
RAHU / KETU												

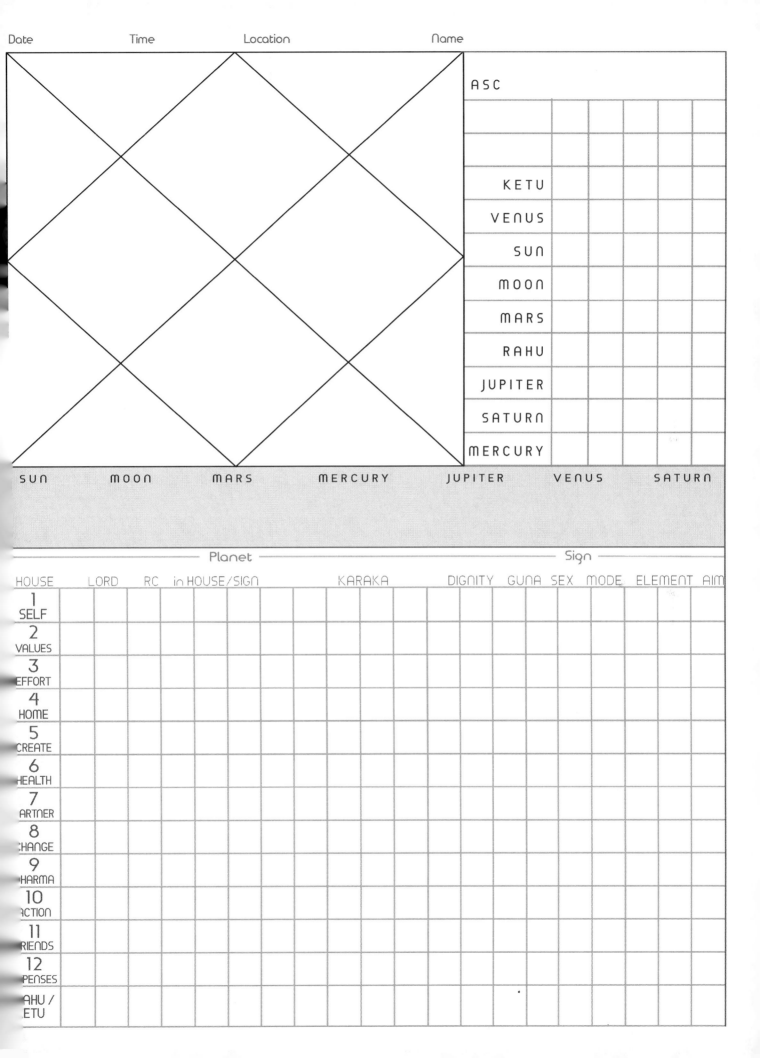

Date	Time	Location	Name

ASC

KETU					
VENUS					
SUN					
MOON					
MARS					
RAHU					
JUPITER					
SATURN					
MERCURY					

SUN	MOON	MARS	MERCURY	JUPITER	VENUS	SATURN

Planet ———————————————— Sign

HOUSE	LORD	RC	in HOUSE/SIGN	KARAKA	DIGNITY	GUNA	SEX	MODE	ELEMENT	AIM
1 SELF										
2 VALUES										
3 EFFORT										
4 HOME										
5 CREATE										
6 HEALTH										
7 PARTNER										
8 CHANGE										
9 DHARMA										
10 ACTION										
11 FRIENDS										
12 EXPENSES										
RAHU / KETU										

Date	Time	Location	Name

ASC

KETU					
VENUS					
SUN					
MOON					
MARS					
RAHU					
JUPITER					
SATURN					
MERCURY					

SUN	MOON	MARS	MERCURY	JUPITER	VENUS	SATURN

Planet ——————————————————— Sign

HOUSE	LORD	RC	in HOUSE/SIGN			KARAKA		DIGNITY	GUNA	SEX	MODE	ELEMENT	AIM
1 SELF													
2 VALUES													
3 EFFORT													
4 HOME													
5 CREATE													
6 HEALTH													
7 PARTNER													
8 CHANGE													
9 DHARMA													
10 ACTION													
11 FRIENDS													
12 EXPENSES													
RAHU / KETU													

Date	Time	Location	Name			

ASC

KETU

VENUS

SUN

MOON

MARS

RAHU

JUPITER

SATURN

MERCURY

SUN	MOON	MARS	MERCURY	JUPITER	VENUS	SATURN

——————————— Planet ——————————— Sign ———————————

HOUSE	LORD	RC	in HOUSE/SIGN	KARAKA	DIGNITY	GUNA	SEX	MODE	ELEMENT	AIM
1 SELF										
2 VALUES										
3 EFFORT										
4 HOME										
5 CREATE										
6 HEALTH										
7 PARTNER										
8 CHANGE										
9 DHARMA										
10 ACTION										
11 FRIENDS										
12 EXPENSES										
RAHU / KETU										

Date   Time   Location   Name

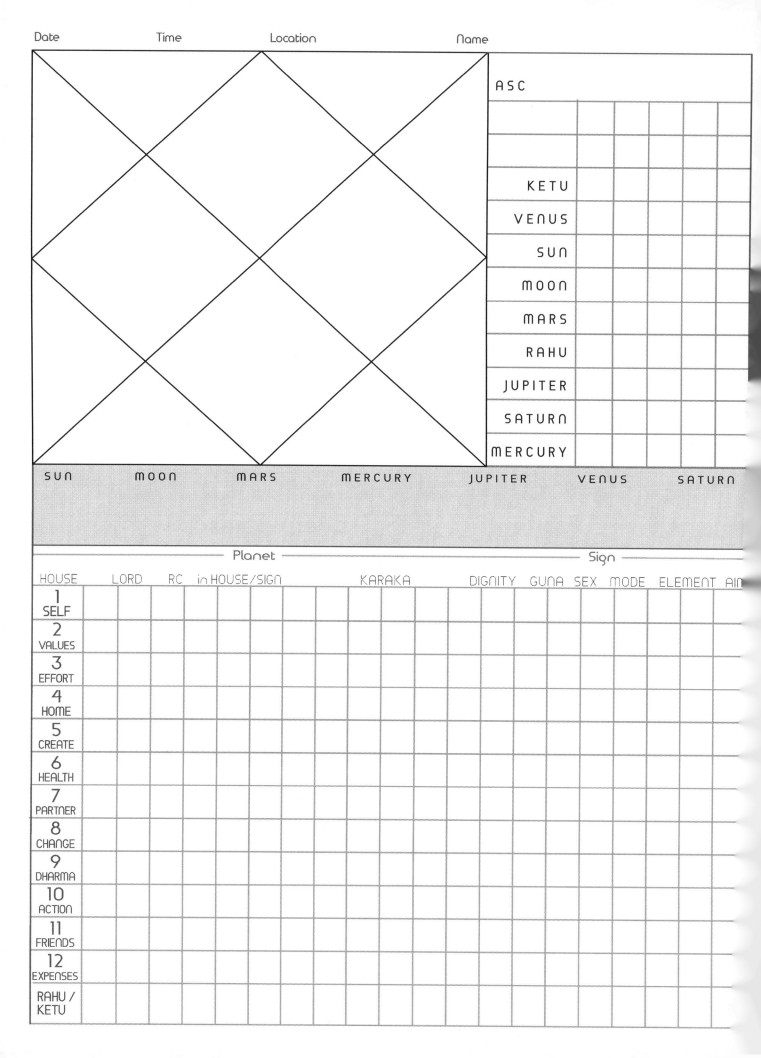

ASC

KETU					
VENUS					
SUN					
MOON					
MARS					
RAHU					
JUPITER					
SATURN					
MERCURY					

SUN	MOON	MARS	MERCURY	JUPITER	VENUS	SATURN

—————— Planet ——————   —————— Sign ——————

HOUSE	LORD	RC	in HOUSE/SIGN			KARAKA		DIGNITY	GUNA	SEX	MODE	ELEMENT	AIM
1 SELF													
2 VALUES													
3 EFFORT													
4 HOME													
5 CREATE													
6 HEALTH													
7 PARTNER													
8 CHANGE													
9 DHARMA													
10 ACTION													
11 FRIENDS													
12 EXPENSES													
RAHU / KETU													

Date	Time	Location	Name

ASC

KETU					
VENUS					
SUN					
MOON					
MARS					
RAHU					
JUPITER					
SATURN					
MERCURY					

SUN	MOON	MARS	MERCURY	JUPITER	VENUS	SATURN

Planet ———————————————————————————— Sign

HOUSE	LORD	RC	in HOUSE/SIGN	KARAKA	DIGNITY	GUNA	SEX	MODE	ELEMENT	AIM
1 SELF										
2 VALUES										
3 EFFORT										
4 HOME										
5 CREATE										
6 HEALTH										
7 PARTNER										
8 CHANGE										
9 DHARMA										
10 ACTION										
11 FRIENDS										
12 EXPENSES										
RAHU / KETU										

Date	Time	Location	Name

ASC

KETU

VENUS

SUN

MOON

MARS

RAHU

JUPITER

SATURN

MERCURY

SUN	MOON	MARS	MERCURY	JUPITER	VENUS	SATURN

Planet ——————————————————————————————— Sign

HOUSE	LORD	RC	in HOUSE/SIGN	KARAKA	DIGNITY	GUNA	SEX	MODE	ELEMENT	AIM
1 SELF										
2 VALUES										
3 EFFORT										
4 HOME										
5 CREATE										
6 HEALTH										
7 PARTNER										
8 CHANGE										
9 DHARMA										
10 ACTION										
11 FRIENDS										
12 EXPENSES										
RAHU / KETU										

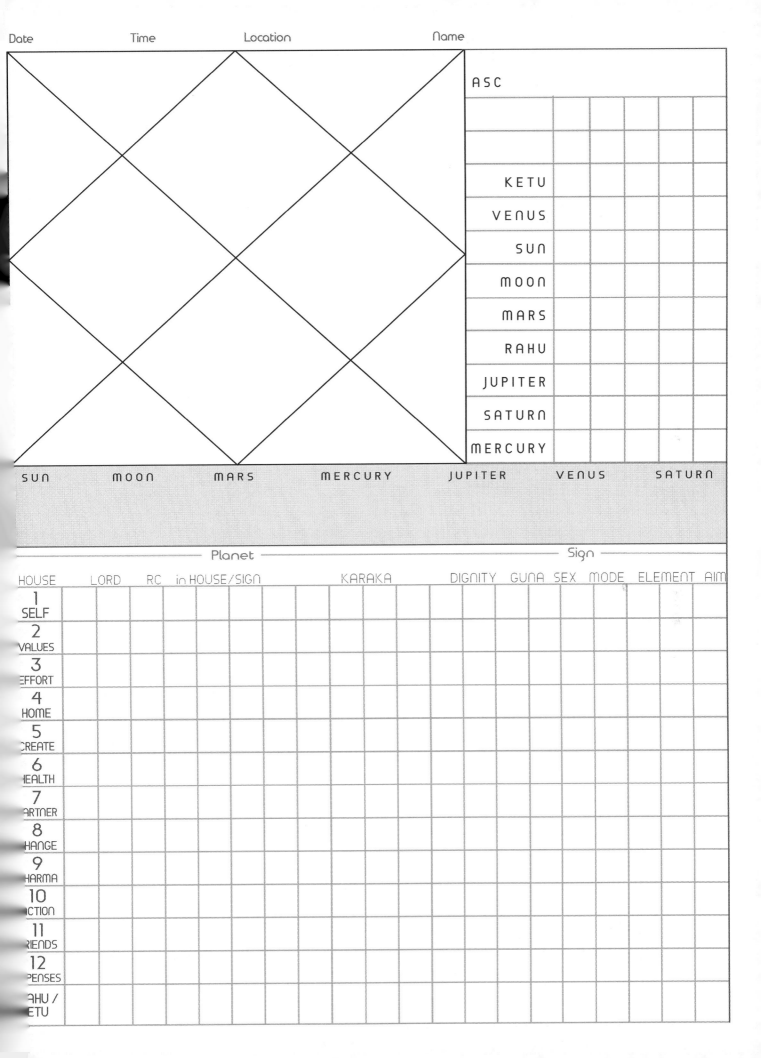

Date   Time   Location   Name

ASC

KETU

VENUS

SUN

MOON

MARS

RAHU

JUPITER

SATURN

MERCURY

SUN	MOON	MARS	MERCURY	JUPITER	VENUS	SATURN

Planet ———————————————— Sign

HOUSE	LORD	RC	in HOUSE/SIGN			KARAKA		DIGNITY	GUNA	SEX	MODE	ELEMENT	AIM
1 SELF													
2 VALUES													
3 EFFORT													
4 HOME													
5 CREATE													
6 HEALTH													
7 PARTNER													
8 CHANGE													
9 DHARMA													
10 ACTION													
11 FRIENDS													
12 EXPENSES													
RAHU / KETU													

ASC

KETU

VENUS

SUN

MOON

MARS

RAHU

JUPITER

SATURN

MERCURY

SUN	MOON	MARS	MERCURY	JUPITER	VENUS	SATURN

	Planet					Sign					
HOUSE	LORD	RC	in HOUSE/SIGN		KARAKA		DIGNITY	GUNA	SEX	MODE	ELEMENT	AIR
1 SELF												
2 VALUES												
3 EFFORT												
4 HOME												
5 CREATE												
6 HEALTH												
7 PARTNER												
8 CHANGE												
9 DHARMA												
10 ACTION												
11 FRIENDS												
12 EXPENSES												
RAHU / KETU												

ASC

KETU

VENUS

SUN

MOON

MARS

RAHU

JUPITER

SATURN

MERCURY

| SUN | MOON | MARS | MERCURY | JUPITER | VENUS | SATURN |

──── Planet ────   ──── Sign ────

HOUSE	LORD	RC	in HOUSE/SIGN				KARAKA		DIGNITY	GUNA	SEX	MODE	ELEMENT	AIM
1 SELF														
2 VALUES														
3 EFFORT														
4 HOME														
5 CREATE														
6 HEALTH														
7 PARTNER														
8 CHANGE														
9 DHARMA														
10 ACTION														
11 FRIENDS														
12 EXPENSES														
RAHU / KETU														

Date	Time	Location	Name

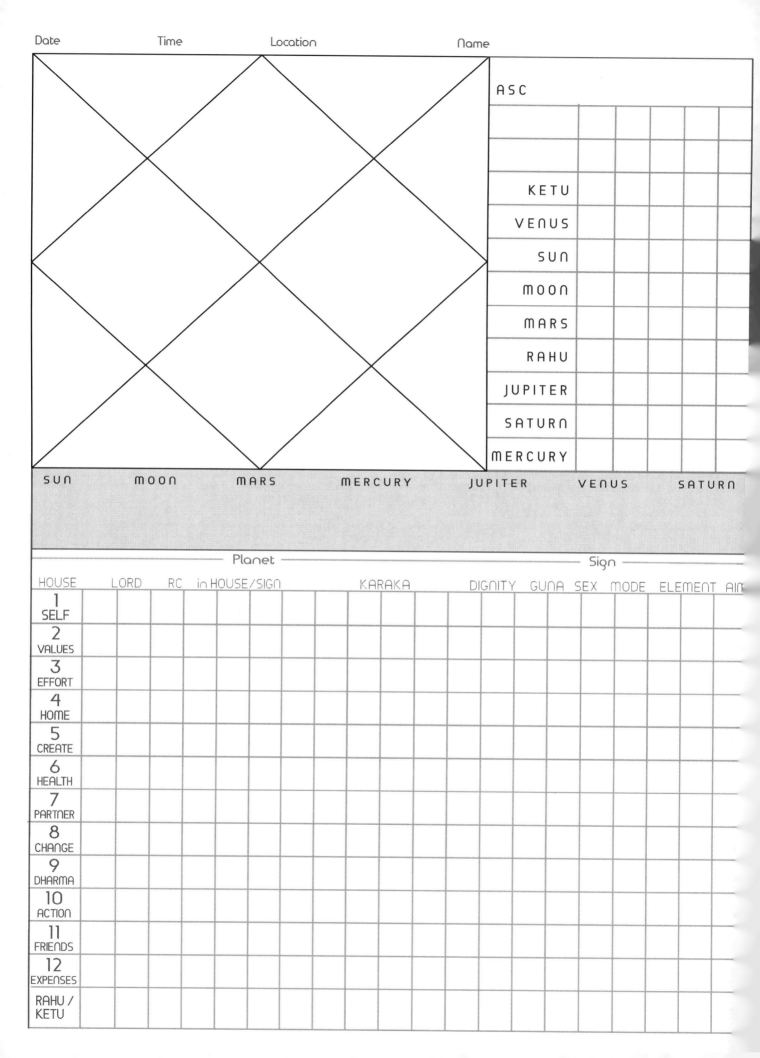

ASC

| KETU |
| VENUS |
| SUN |
| MOON |
| MARS |
| RAHU |
| JUPITER |
| SATURN |
| MERCURY |

SUN	MOON	MARS	MERCURY	JUPITER	VENUS	SATURN

Planet — Sign

HOUSE	LORD	RC	in HOUSE/SIGN	KARAKA	DIGNITY	GUNA	SEX	MODE	ELEMENT	AIM
1 SELF										
2 VALUES										
3 EFFORT										
4 HOME										
5 CREATE										
6 HEALTH										
7 PARTNER										
8 CHANGE										
9 DHARMA										
10 ACTION										
11 FRIENDS										
12 EXPENSES										
RAHU / KETU										

Date	Time	Location	Name

	ASC

KETU
VENUS
SUN
MOON
MARS
RAHU
JUPITER
SATURN
MERCURY

SUN	MOON	MARS	MERCURY	JUPITER	VENUS	SATURN

Planet —————————————————————————— Sign

HOUSE	LORD	RC	in HOUSE/SIGN			KARAKA			DIGNITY	GUNA	SEX	MODE	ELEMENT	AIM
1 SELF														
2 VALUES														
3 EFFORT														
4 HOME														
5 CREATE														
6 HEALTH														
7 PARTNER														
8 CHANGE														
9 DHARMA														
10 ACTION														
11 FRIENDS														
12 EXPENSES														
RAHU / KETU														

Date	Time	Location	Name

ASC

KETU					
VENUS					
SUN					
MOON					
MARS					
RAHU					
JUPITER					
SATURN					
MERCURY					

SUN	MOON	MARS	MERCURY	JUPITER	VENUS	SATURN

Planet						Sign					
HOUSE	LORD	RC	in HOUSE/SIGN		KARAKA	DIGNITY	GUNA	SEX	MODE	ELEMENT	AIR
1 SELF											
2 VALUES											
3 EFFORT											
4 HOME											
5 CREATE											
6 HEALTH											
7 PARTNER											
8 CHANGE											
9 DHARMA											
10 ACTION											
11 FRIENDS											
12 EXPENSES											
RAHU / KETU											

Date　　　　　Time　　　　　Location　　　　　Name

ASC

KETU					
VENUS					
SUN					
MOON					
MARS					
RAHU					
JUPITER					
SATURN					
MERCURY					

SUN	MOON	MARS	MERCURY	JUPITER	VENUS	SATURN

——— Planet ———　　　　　　　——— Sign ———

HOUSE	LORD	RC	in HOUSE/SIGN	KARAKA	DIGNITY	GUNA	SEX	MODE	ELEMENT	AIM
1 SELF										
2 VALUES										
3 EFFORT										
4 HOME										
5 CREATE										
6 HEALTH										
7 PARTNER										
8 CHANGE										
9 DHARMA										
10 ACTION										
11 FRIENDS										
12 EXPENSES										
RAHU / KETU										

Date   Time   Location   Name

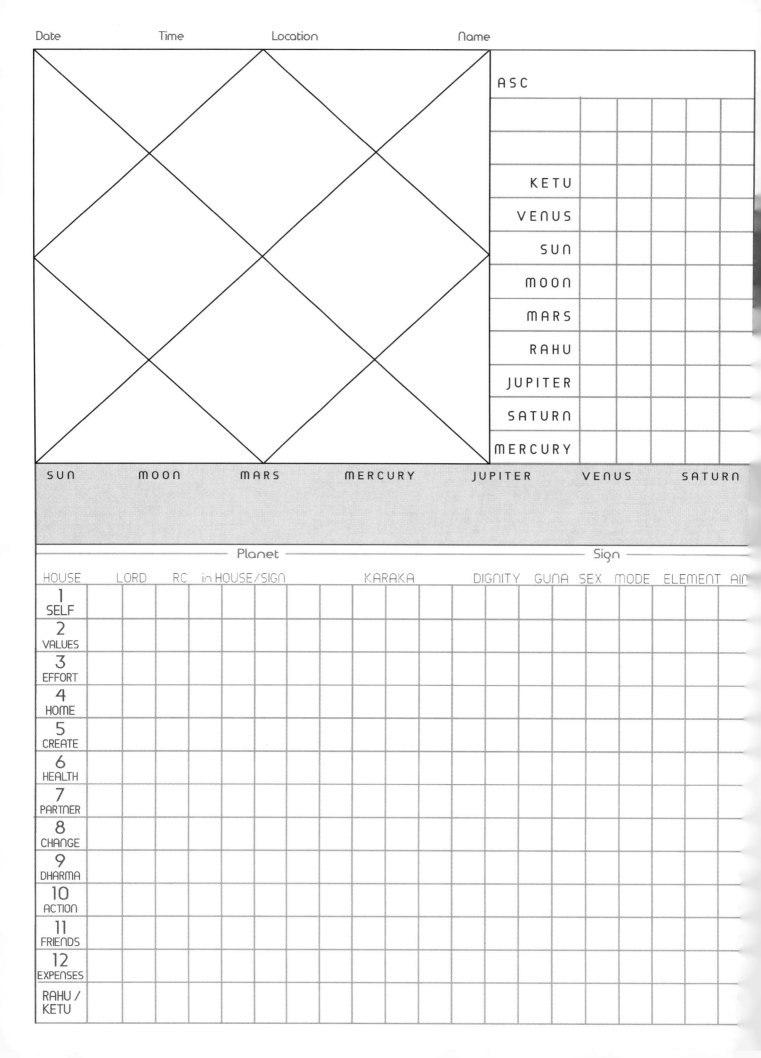

ASC

| KETU |
| VENUS |
| SUN |
| MOON |
| MARS |
| RAHU |
| JUPITER |
| SATURN |
| MERCURY |

| SUN | MOON | MARS | MERCURY | JUPITER | VENUS | SATURN |

Planet   Sign

HOUSE	LORD	RC	in HOUSE/SIGN				KARAKA			DIGNITY	GUNA	SEX	MODE	ELEMENT	AIR
1 SELF															
2 VALUES															
3 EFFORT															
4 HOME															
5 CREATE															
6 HEALTH															
7 PARTNER															
8 CHANGE															
9 DHARMA															
10 ACTION															
11 FRIENDS															
12 EXPENSES															
RAHU / KETU															

Date	Time	Location	Name

ASC

| KETU |
| VENUS |
| SUN |
| MOON |
| MARS |
| RAHU |
| JUPITER |
| SATURN |
| MERCURY |

SUN	MOON	MARS	MERCURY	JUPITER	VENUS	SATURN

―――― Planet ――――　　　　　　　　　―――― Sign ――――

HOUSE	LORD	RC	in HOUSE/SIGN	KARAKA	DIGNITY	GUNA	SEX	MODE	ELEMENT	AIM
1 SELF										
2 VALUES										
3 EFFORT										
4 HOME										
5 CREATE										
6 HEALTH										
7 PARTNER										
8 CHANGE										
9 DHARMA										
10 ACTION										
11 FRIENDS										
12 EXPENSES										
RAHU / KETU										

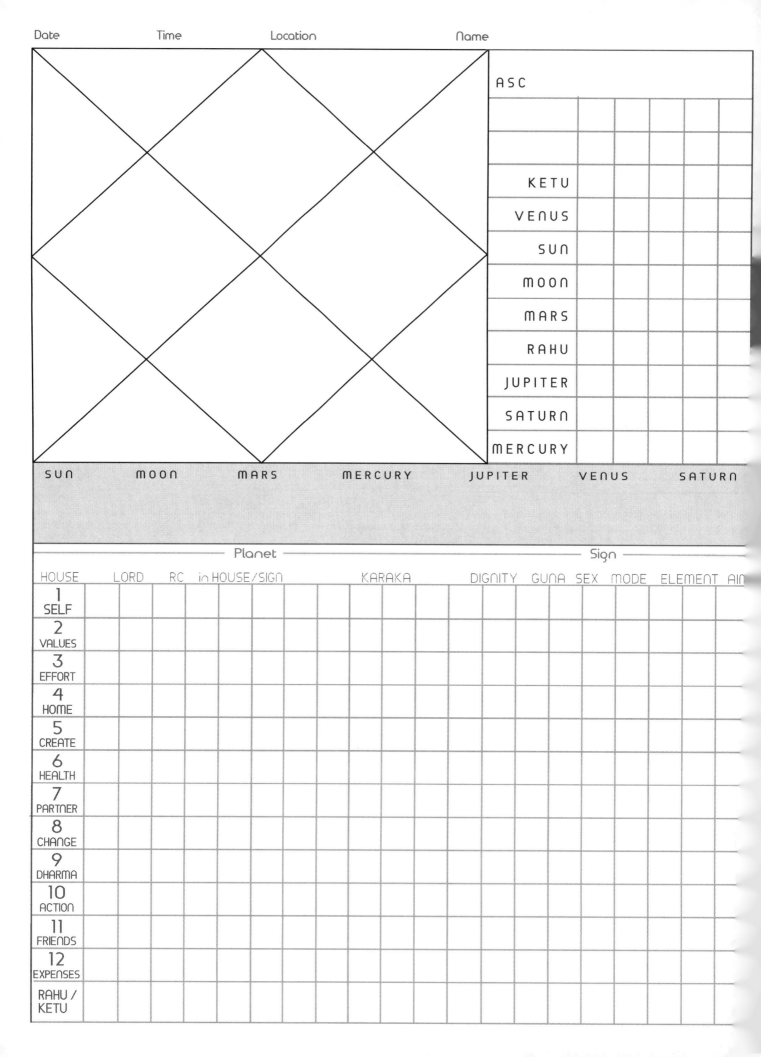

Date	Time	Location	Name

ASC

KETU					
VENUS					
SUN					
MOON					
MARS					
RAHU					
JUPITER					
SATURN					
MERCURY					

SUN	MOON	MARS	MERCURY	JUPITER	VENUS	SATURN

——— Planet ———   ——— Sign ———

HOUSE	LORD	RC	in HOUSE/SIGN				KARAKA		DIGNITY	GUNA	SEX	MODE	ELEMENT	AIM
1 SELF														
2 VALUES														
3 EFFORT														
4 HOME														
5 CREATE														
6 HEALTH														
7 PARTNER														
8 CHANGE														
9 DHARMA														
10 ACTION														
11 FRIENDS														
12 EXPENSES														
RAHU / KETU														

ASC

KETU					
VENUS					
SUN					
MOON					
MARS					
RAHU					
JUPITER					
SATURN					
MERCURY					

SUN	MOON	MARS	MERCURY	JUPITER	VENUS	SATURN

	— Planet —					— Sign —				
HOUSE	LORD	RC	in HOUSE/SIGN		KARAKA	DIGNITY	GUNA	SEX	MODE	ELEMENT	AIM
1 SELF											
2 VALUES											
3 EFFORT											
4 HOME											
5 CREATE											
6 HEALTH											
7 PARTNER											
8 CHANGE											
9 DHARMA											
10 ACTION											
11 FRIENDS											
12 EXPENSES											
RAHU / KETU											

Date   Time   Location   Name

ASC

| KETU |
| VENUS |
| SUN |
| MOON |
| MARS |
| RAHU |
| JUPITER |
| SATURN |
| MERCURY |

SUN	MOON	MARS	MERCURY	JUPITER	VENUS	SATURN

──── Planet ────   ──── Sign ────

HOUSE	LORD	RC	in HOUSE/SIGN	KARAKA	DIGNITY	GUNA	SEX	MODE	ELEMENT	AIR
1 SELF										
2 VALUES										
3 EFFORT										
4 HOME										
5 CREATE										
6 HEALTH										
7 PARTNER										
8 CHANGE										
9 DHARMA										
10 ACTION										
11 FRIENDS										
12 EXPENSES										
RAHU / KETU										

Date   Time   Location   Name

ASC

KETU					
VENUS					
SUN					
MOON					
MARS					
RAHU					
JUPITER					
SATURN					
MERCURY					

SUN   MOON   MARS   MERCURY   JUPITER   VENUS   SATURN

———————————————— Planet ————————————————   ———————— Sign ————————

HOUSE	LORD	RC	in HOUSE/SIGN			KARAKA		DIGNITY	GUNA	SEX	MODE	ELEMENT	AIM
1 SELF													
2 VALUES													
3 EFFORT													
4 HOME													
5 CREATE													
6 HEALTH													
7 PARTNER													
8 CHANGE													
9 DHARMA													
10 ACTION													
11 FRIENDS													
12 EXPENSES													
RAHU / KETU													

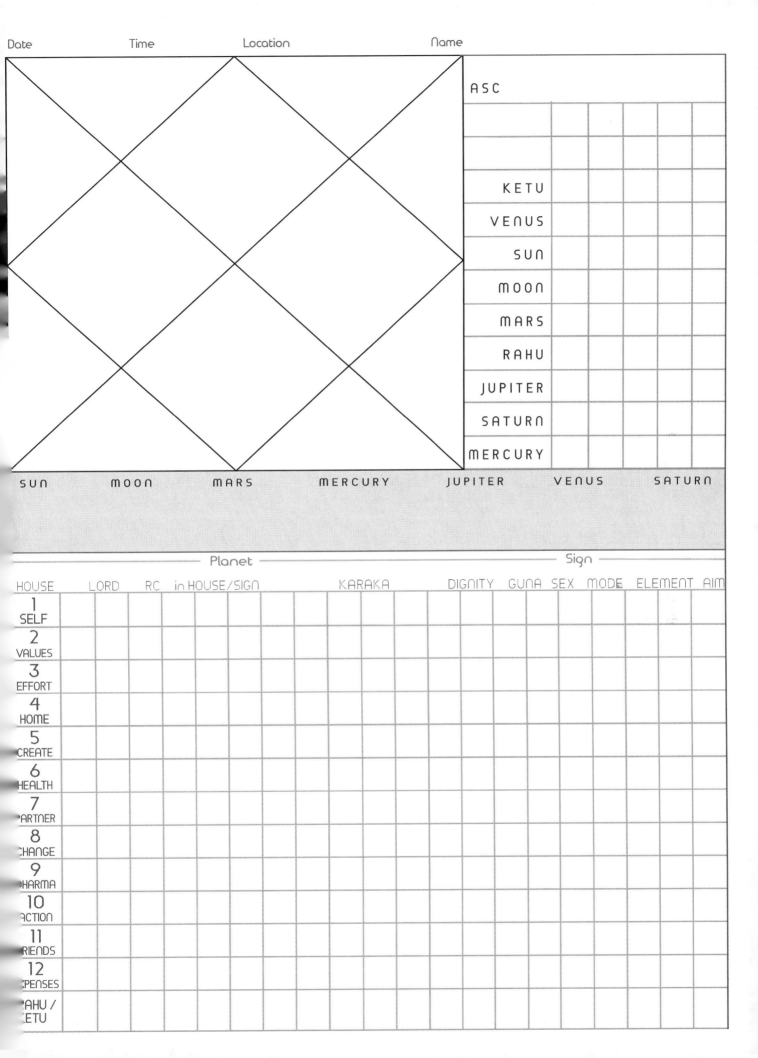

Date	Time	Location	Name

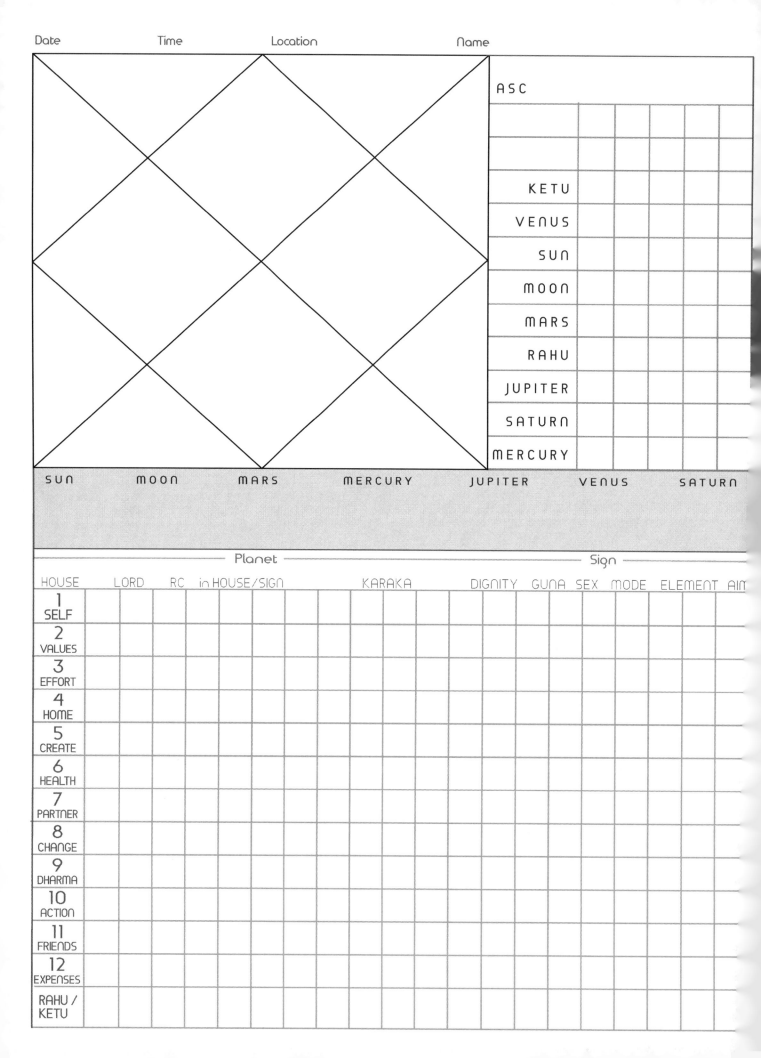

ASC

| KETU |
| VENUS |
| SUN |
| MOON |
| MARS |
| RAHU |
| JUPITER |
| SATURN |
| MERCURY |

SUN	MOON	MARS	MERCURY	JUPITER	VENUS	SATURN

—————— Planet —————————————————————— Sign ——————

HOUSE	LORD	RC	in HOUSE/SIGN	KARAKA	DIGNITY	GUNA	SEX	MODE	ELEMENT	AIM
1 SELF										
2 VALUES										
3 EFFORT										
4 HOME										
5 CREATE										
6 HEALTH										
7 PARTNER										
8 CHANGE										
9 DHARMA										
10 ACTION										
11 FRIENDS										
12 EXPENSES										
RAHU / KETU										

Date	Time	Location	Name

ASC

KETU				
VENUS				
SUN				
MOON				
MARS				
RAHU				
JUPITER				
SATURN				
MERCURY				

SUN	MOON	MARS	MERCURY	JUPITER	VENUS	SATURN

—— Planet ——   —— Sign ——

HOUSE	LORD	RC	in HOUSE/SIGN	KARAKA	DIGNITY	GUNA	SEX	MODE	ELEMENT	AIM
1 SELF										
2 VALUES										
3 EFFORT										
4 HOME										
5 CREATE										
6 HEALTH										
7 PARTNER										
8 CHANGE										
9 DHARMA										
10 ACTION										
11 FRIENDS										
12 EXPENSES										
RAHU / KETU										

Date		Time		Location		Name	

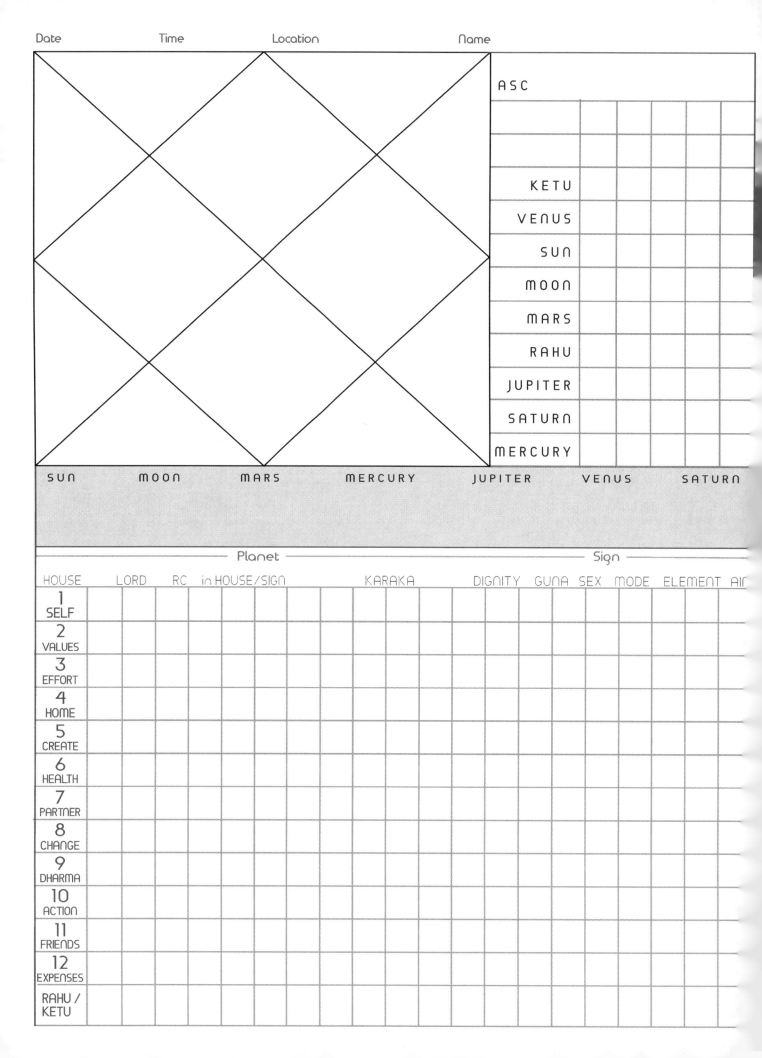

ASC

KETU						
VENUS						
SUN						
MOON						
MARS						
RAHU						
JUPITER						
SATURN						
MERCURY						

SUN	MOON	MARS	MERCURY	JUPITER	VENUS	SATURN

Planet ———————————————————————— Sign

HOUSE	LORD	RC	in HOUSE/SIGN		KARAKA		DIGNITY	GUNA	SEX	MODE	ELEMENT	AIR
1 SELF												
2 VALUES												
3 EFFORT												
4 HOME												
5 CREATE												
6 HEALTH												
7 PARTNER												
8 CHANGE												
9 DHARMA												
10 ACTION												
11 FRIENDS												
12 EXPENSES												
RAHU / KETU												

Date   Time   Location   Name

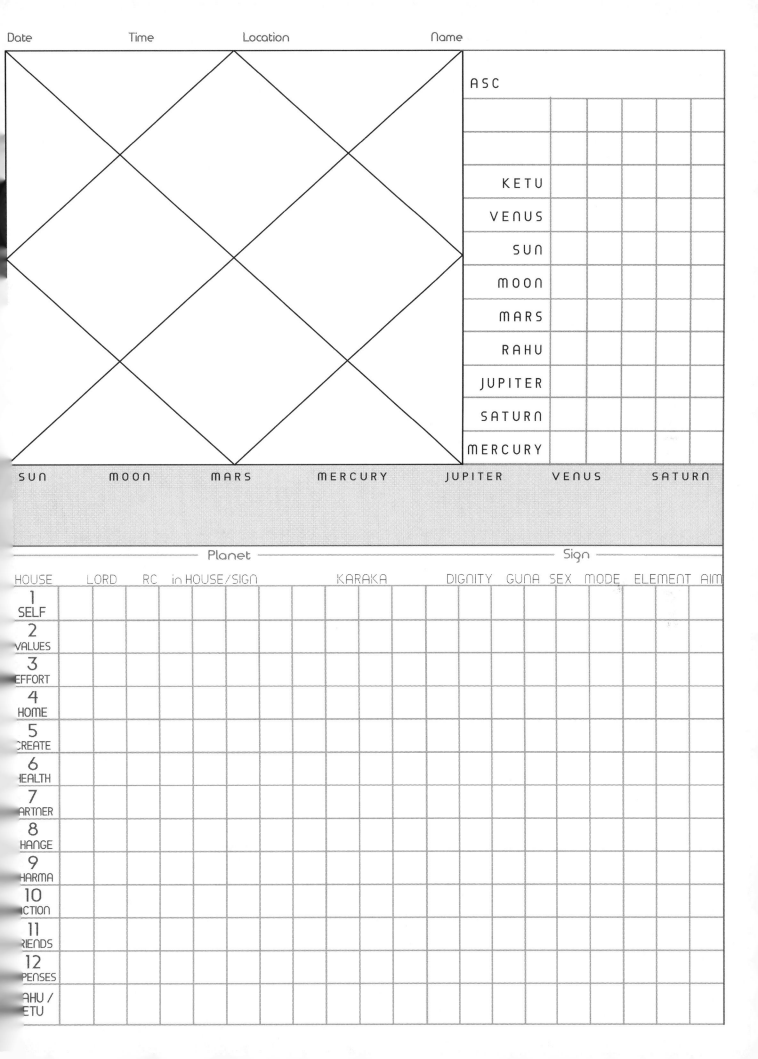

ASC

KETU

VENUS

SUN

MOON

MARS

RAHU

JUPITER

SATURN

MERCURY

SUN   MOON   MARS   MERCURY   JUPITER   VENUS   SATURN

———— Planet ————   ———— Sign ————

HOUSE	LORD	RC	in HOUSE/SIGN	KARAKA	DIGNITY	GUNA	SEX	MODE	ELEMENT	AIM
1 SELF										
2 VALUES										
3 EFFORT										
4 HOME										
5 CREATE										
6 HEALTH										
7 PARTNER										
8 CHANGE										
9 DHARMA										
10 ACTION										
11 FRIENDS										
12 EXPENSES										
RAHU / KETU										

Date   Time   Location   Name

ASC

KETU

VENUS

SUN

MOON

MARS

RAHU

JUPITER

SATURN

MERCURY

| SUN | MOON | MARS | MERCURY | JUPITER | VENUS | SATURN |

Planet   Sign

HOUSE	LORD	RC	in HOUSE/SIGN	KARAKA	DIGNITY	GUNA	SEX	MODE	ELEMENT	F
1 SELF										
2 VALUES										
3 EFFORT										
4 HOME										
5 CREATE										
6 HEALTH										
7 PARTNER										
8 CHANGE										
9 DHARMA										
10 ACTION										
11 FRIENDS										
12 EXPENSES										
RAHU / KETU										

Date	Time	Location	Name

ASC

KETU

VENUS

SUN

MOON

MARS

RAHU

JUPITER

SATURN

MERCURY

SUN	MOON	MARS	MERCURY	JUPITER	VENUS	SATURN

―――――― Planet ―――――― ―――――― Sign ――――――

HOUSE	LORD	RC	in HOUSE/SIGN		KARAKA		DIGNITY	GUNA	SEX	MODE	ELEMENT	AIM
1 SELF												
2 VALUES												
3 EFFORT												
4 HOME												
5 CREATE												
6 HEALTH												
7 PARTNER												
8 CHANGE												
9 DHARMA												
10 ACTION												
11 FRIENDS												
12 EXPENSES												
RAHU / KETU												

Date	Time	Location	Name

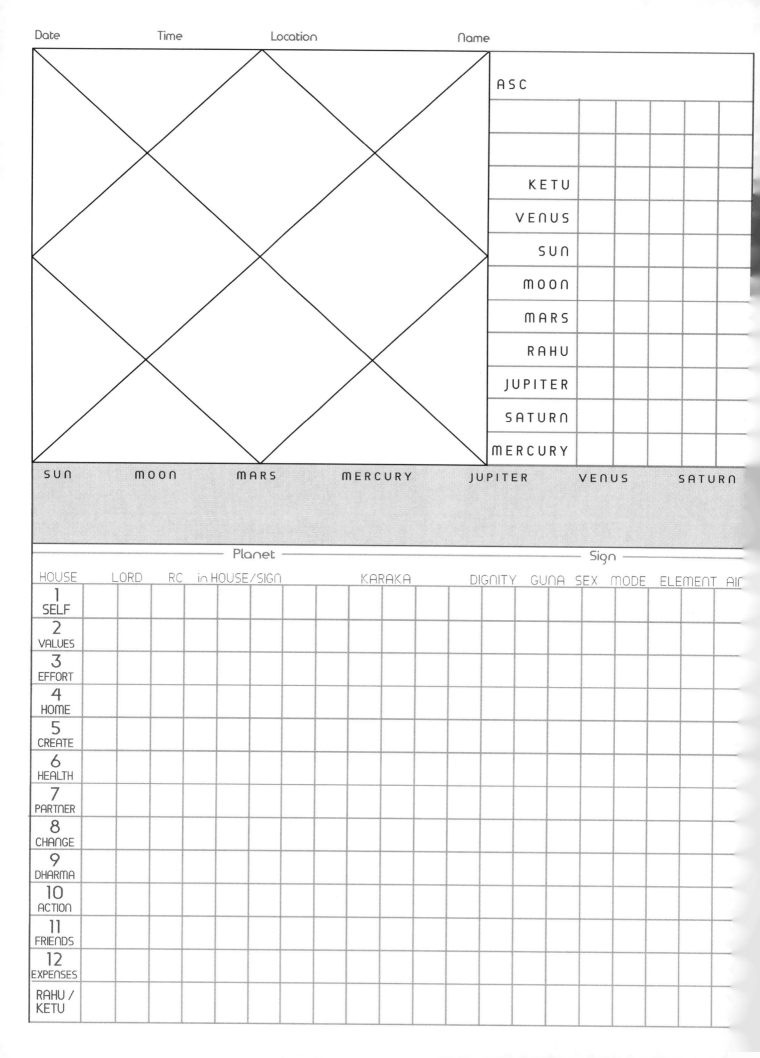

ASC

KETU

VENUS

SUN

MOON

MARS

RAHU

JUPITER

SATURN

MERCURY

SUN	MOON	MARS	MERCURY	JUPITER	VENUS	SATURN

──── Planet ──── ──── Sign ────

HOUSE	LORD	RC	in HOUSE/SIGN	KARAKA	DIGNITY	GUNA	SEX	MODE	ELEMENT	AIR
1 SELF										
2 VALUES										
3 EFFORT										
4 HOME										
5 CREATE										
6 HEALTH										
7 PARTNER										
8 CHANGE										
9 DHARMA										
10 ACTION										
11 FRIENDS										
12 EXPENSES										
RAHU / KETU										

Date   Time   Location   Name

ASC

KETU

VENUS

SUN

MOON

MARS

RAHU

JUPITER

SATURN

MERCURY

SUN	MOON	MARS	MERCURY	JUPITER	VENUS	SATURN

———— Planet ————   ———— Sign ————

HOUSE	LORD	RC	in HOUSE/SIGN	KARAKA	DIGNITY	GUNA	SEX	MODE	ELEMENT	AIM
1 SELF										
2 VALUES										
3 EFFORT										
4 HOME										
5 CREATE										
6 HEALTH										
7 PARTNER										
8 CHANGE										
9 DHARMA										
10 ACTION										
11 FRIENDS										
12 EXPENSES										
RAHU / KETU										

Date	Time	Location	Name

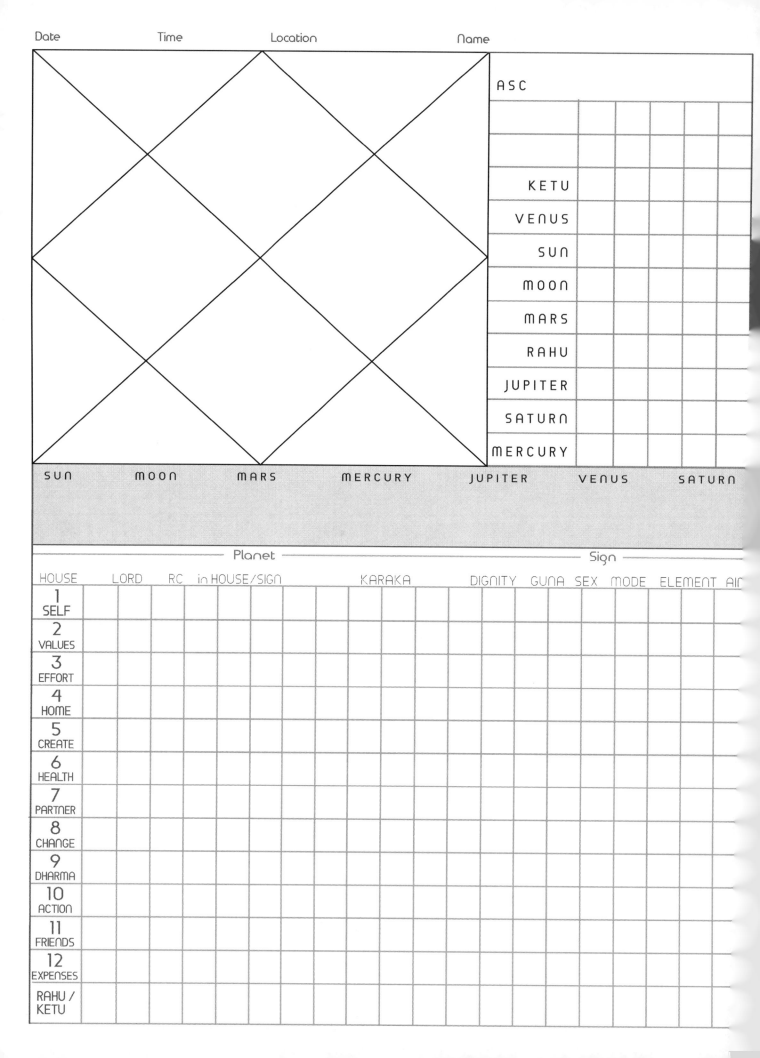

ASC

KETU
VENUS
SUN
MOON
MARS
RAHU
JUPITER
SATURN
MERCURY

SUN	MOON	MARS	MERCURY	JUPITER	VENUS	SATURN

Planet ——————————————— Sign

HOUSE	LORD	RC	in HOUSE/SIGN	KARAKA	DIGNITY	GUNA	SEX	MODE	ELEMENT	AIR
1 SELF										
2 VALUES										
3 EFFORT										
4 HOME										
5 CREATE										
6 HEALTH										
7 PARTNER										
8 CHANGE										
9 DHARMA										
10 ACTION										
11 FRIENDS										
12 EXPENSES										
RAHU / KETU										

Date	Time	Location	Name

ASC

KETU				
VENUS				
SUN				
MOON				
MARS				
RAHU				
JUPITER				
SATURN				
MERCURY				

SUN	MOON	MARS	MERCURY	JUPITER	VENUS	SATURN

─── Planet ─── ─── Sign ───

HOUSE	LORD	RC	in HOUSE/SIGN	KARAKA	DIGNITY	GUNA	SEX	MODE	ELEMENT	AIM
1 SELF										
2 VALUES										
3 EFFORT										
4 HOME										
5 CREATE										
6 HEALTH										
7 PARTNER										
8 CHANGE										
9 DHARMA										
10 ACTION										
11 FRIENDS										
12 EXPENSES										
RAHU / KETU										

Date	Time	Location	Name

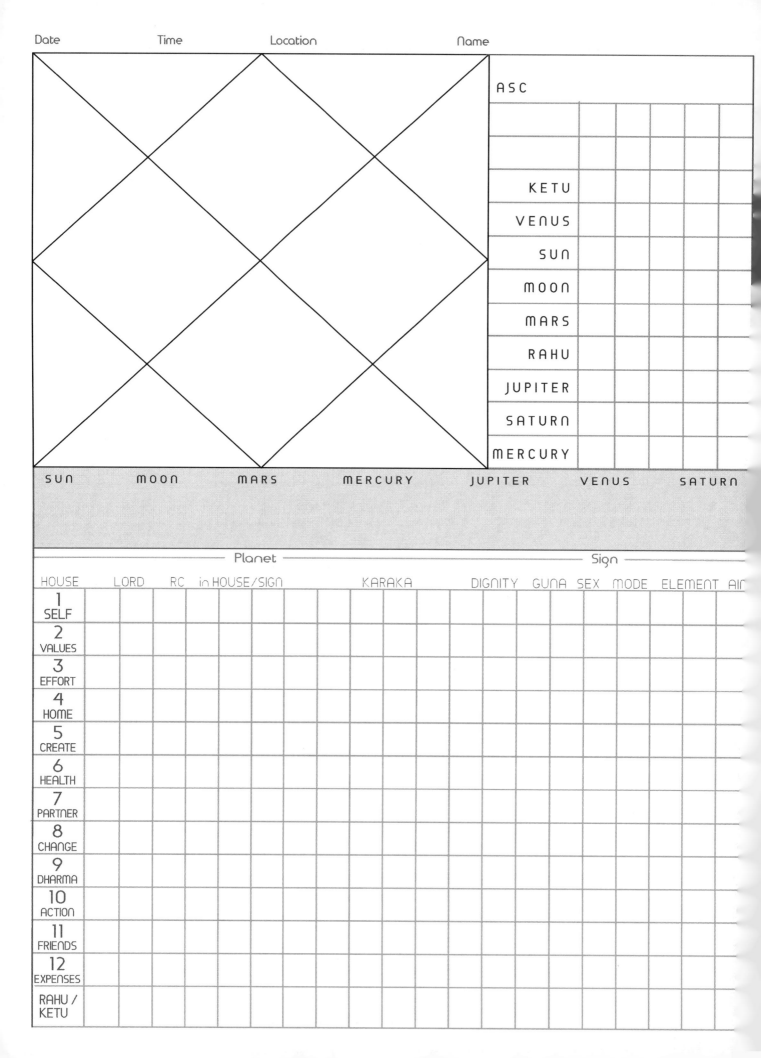

ASC

KETU

VENUS

SUN

MOON

MARS

RAHU

JUPITER

SATURN

MERCURY

SUN	MOON	MARS	MERCURY	JUPITER	VENUS	SATURN

Planet — Sign

HOUSE	LORD	RC	in HOUSE/SIGN	KARAKA	DIGNITY	GUNA	SEX	MODE	ELEMENT	AIR
1 SELF										
2 VALUES										
3 EFFORT										
4 HOME										
5 CREATE										
6 HEALTH										
7 PARTNER										
8 CHANGE										
9 DHARMA										
10 ACTION										
11 FRIENDS										
12 EXPENSES										
RAHU / KETU										

Date   Time   Location   Name

ASC

KETU

VENUS

SUN

MOON

MARS

RAHU

JUPITER

SATURN

MERCURY

SUN   MOON   MARS   MERCURY   JUPITER   VENUS   SATURN

Planet ———————————————————————— Sign

HOUSE	LORD	RC	in HOUSE/SIGN	KARAKA	DIGNITY	GUNA	SEX	MODE	ELEMENT	AIM
1 SELF										
2 VALUES										
3 EFFORT										
4 HOME										
5 CREATE										
6 HEALTH										
7 PARTNER										
8 CHANGE										
9 DHARMA										
10 ACTION										
11 FRIENDS										
12 EXPENSES										
RAHU / KETU										

Date	Time	Location	Name

ASC

KETU					
VENUS					
SUN					
MOON					
MARS					
RAHU					
JUPITER					
SATURN					
MERCURY					

SUN	MOON	MARS	MERCURY	JUPITER	VENUS	SATURN

—— Planet ————————————————————————————— Sign ——

HOUSE	LORD	RC	in HOUSE/SIGN				KARAKA		DIGNITY	GUNA	SEX	MODE	ELEMENT	AIR
1 SELF														
2 VALUES														
3 EFFORT														
4 HOME														
5 CREATE														
6 HEALTH														
7 PARTNER														
8 CHANGE														
9 DHARMA														
10 ACTION														
11 FRIENDS														
12 EXPENSES														
RAHU / KETU														

Date	Time	Location	Name

ASC

KETU					
VENUS					
SUN					
MOON					
MARS					
RAHU					
JUPITER					
SATURN					
MERCURY					

SUN	MOON	MARS	MERCURY	JUPITER	VENUS	SATURN

— Planet — — Sign —

HOUSE	LORD	RC	in HOUSE/SIGN	KARAKA	DIGNITY	GUNA	SEX	MODE	ELEMENT	AIM
1 SELF										
2 VALUES										
3 EFFORT										
4 HOME										
5 CREATE										
6 HEALTH										
7 PARTNER										
8 CHANGE										
9 DHARMA										
10 ACTION										
11 FRIENDS										
12 EXPENSES										
RAHU / KETU										

ASC

Date	Time	Location	Name

ASC

KETU				
VENUS				
SUN				
MOON				
MARS				
RAHU				
JUPITER				
SATURN				
MERCURY				

SUN	MOON	MARS	MERCURY	JUPITER	VENUS	SATURN

Planet ———————————————— **Sign**

HOUSE	LORD	RC	in HOUSE/SIGN	KARAKA	DIGNITY	GUNA	SEX	MODE	ELEMENT	AIR
1 SELF										
2 VALUES										
3 EFFORT										
4 HOME										
5 CREATE										
6 HEALTH										
7 PARTNER										
8 CHANGE										
9 DHARMA										
10 ACTION										
11 FRIENDS										
12 EXPENSES										
RAHU / KETU										

Date   Time   Location   Name

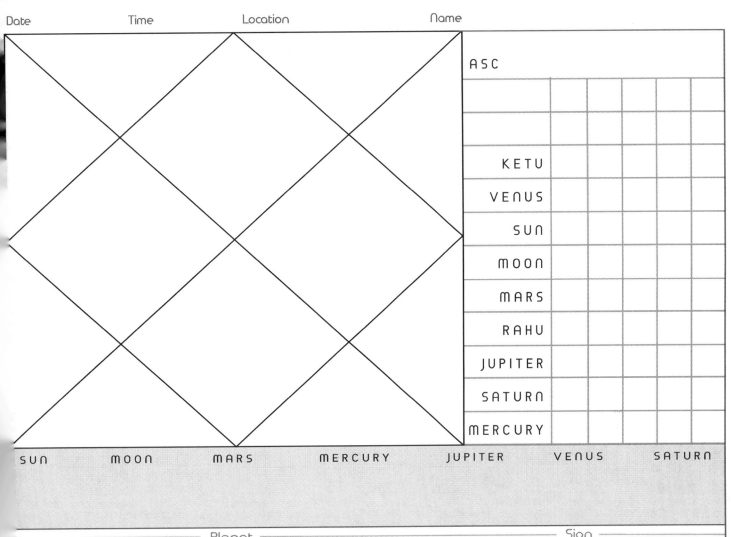

ASC

KETU

VENUS

SUN

MOON

MARS

RAHU

JUPITER

SATURN

MERCURY

SUN   MOON   MARS   MERCURY   JUPITER   VENUS   SATURN

	Planet								Sign						
HOUSE	LORD	RC	in HOUSE/SIGN			KARAKA			DIGNITY	GUNA	SEX	MODE	ELEMENT	AIM	
1 SELF															
2 VALUES															
3 EFFORT															
4 HOME															
5 CREATE															
6 HEALTH															
7 PARTNER															
8 CHANGE															
9 DHARMA															
10 ACTION															
11 FRIENDS															
12 EXPENSES															
RAHU / KETU															

Date   Time   Location   Name

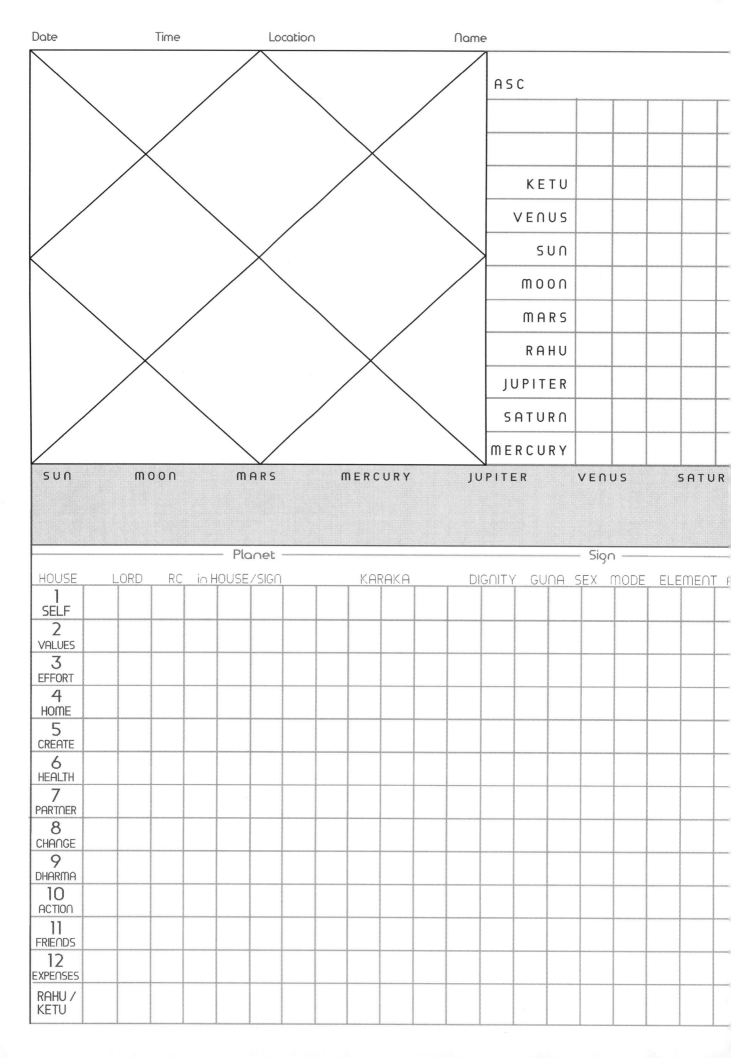

ASC

KETU

VENUS

SUN

MOON

MARS

RAHU

JUPITER

SATURN

MERCURY

SUN   MOON   MARS   MERCURY   JUPITER   VENUS   SATUR

————————— Planet —————————   ————— Sign —————

HOUSE	LORD	RC	in HOUSE/SIGN	KARAKA	DIGNITY	GUNA	SEX	MODE	ELEMENT	
1 SELF										
2 VALUES										
3 EFFORT										
4 HOME										
5 CREATE										
6 HEALTH										
7 PARTNER										
8 CHANGE										
9 DHARMA										
10 ACTION										
11 FRIENDS										
12 EXPENSES										
RAHU / KETU										

Date   Time   Location   Name

ASC						
KETU						
VENUS						
SUN						
MOON						
MARS						
RAHU						
JUPITER						
SATURN						
MERCURY						

SUN   MOON   MARS   MERCURY   JUPITER   VENUS   SATURN

Planet ———————————————————————————— Sign

HOUSE	LORD	RC	in HOUSE/SIGN	KARAKA	DIGNITY	GUNA	SEX	MODE	ELEMENT	AIM
1 SELF										
2 VALUES										
3 EFFORT										
4 HOME										
5 CREATE										
6 HEALTH										
7 PARTNER										
8 CHANGE										
9 DHARMA										
10 ACTION										
11 FRIENDS										
12 EXPENSES										
RAHU / KETU										

Date	Time	Location	Name

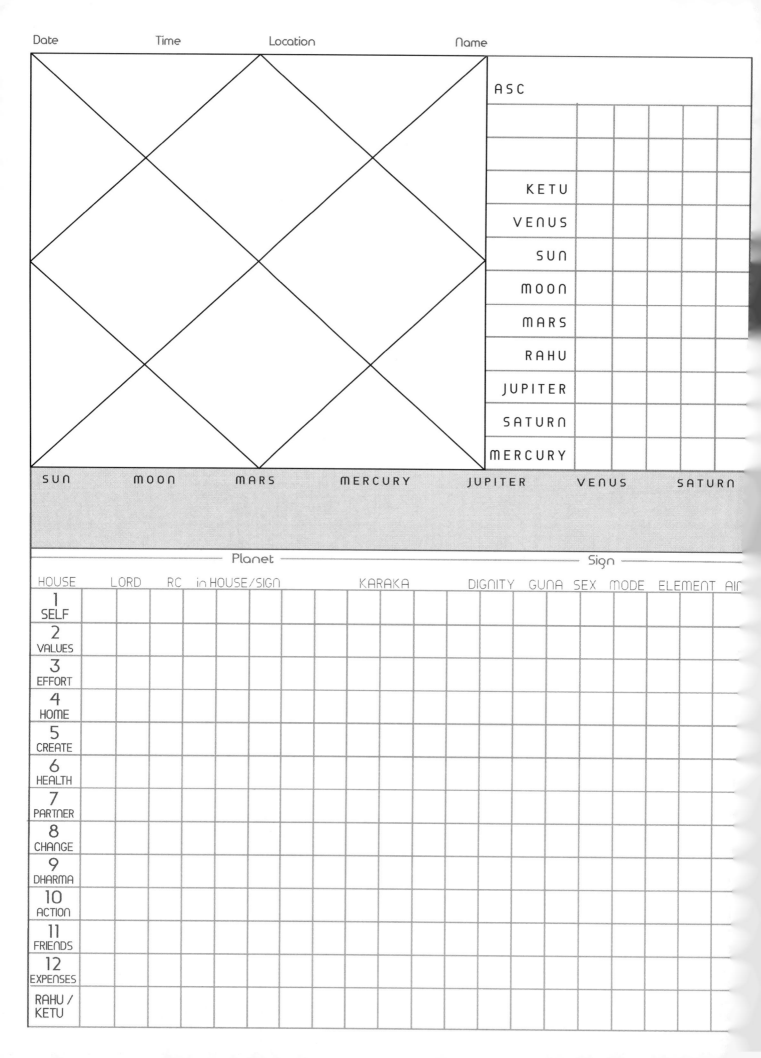

ASC

KETU
VENUS
SUN
MOON
MARS
RAHU
JUPITER
SATURN
MERCURY

SUN	MOON	MARS	MERCURY	JUPITER	VENUS	SATURN

———— Planet ———————————————— Sign ————

HOUSE	LORD	RC	in HOUSE/SIGN	KARAKA	DIGNITY	GUNA	SEX	MODE	ELEMENT	AIR
1 SELF										
2 VALUES										
3 EFFORT										
4 HOME										
5 CREATE										
6 HEALTH										
7 PARTNER										
8 CHANGE										
9 DHARMA										
10 ACTION										
11 FRIENDS										
12 EXPENSES										
RAHU / KETU										

Date	Time	Location	Name

ASC

KETU					
VENUS					
SUN					
MOON					
MARS					
RAHU					
JUPITER					
SATURN					
MERCURY					

SUN	MOON	MARS	MERCURY	JUPITER	VENUS	SATURN

Planet — Sign

HOUSE	LORD	RC	in HOUSE/SIGN	KARAKA	DIGNITY	GUNA	SEX	MODE	ELEMENT	AIM
1 SELF										
2 VALUES										
3 EFFORT										
4 HOME										
5 CREATE										
6 HEALTH										
7 PARTNER										
8 CHANGE										
9 DHARMA										
10 ACTION										
11 FRIENDS										
12 EXPENSES										
RAHU / KETU										

Date	Time	Location	Name

ASC

KETU					
VENUS					
SUN					
MOON					
MARS					
RAHU					
JUPITER					
SATURN					
MERCURY					

SUN	MOON	MARS	MERCURY	JUPITER	VENUS	SATURN

―――――― Planet ――― Sign ――――――

HOUSE	LORD	RC	in HOUSE/SIGN	KARAKA	DIGNITY	GUNA	SEX	MODE	ELEMENT	AIR
1 SELF										
2 VALUES										
3 EFFORT										
4 HOME										
5 CREATE										
6 HEALTH										
7 PARTNER										
8 CHANGE										
9 DHARMA										
10 ACTION										
11 FRIENDS										
12 EXPENSES										
RAHU / KETU										

Date	Time	Location	Name

ASC

KETU						
VENUS						
SUN						
MOON						
MARS						
RAHU						
JUPITER						
SATURN						
MERCURY						

SUN	MOON	MARS	MERCURY	JUPITER	VENUS	SATURN

Planet ──────── **Sign**

HOUSE	LORD	RC	in HOUSE/SIGN	KARAKA	DIGNITY	GUNA	SEX	MODE	ELEMENT	AIM
1 SELF										
2 VALUES										
3 EFFORT										
4 HOME										
5 CREATE										
6 HEALTH										
7 PARTNER										
8 CHANGE										
9 DHARMA										
10 ACTION										
11 FRIENDS										
12 EXPENSES										
RAHU / KETU										

Date	Time	Location	Name

ASC

KETU

VENUS

SUN

MOON

MARS

RAHU

JUPITER

SATURN

MERCURY

SUN	MOON	MARS	MERCURY	JUPITER	VENUS	SATURN

─── Planet ───────────────────────────────── Sign ───

HOUSE	LORD	RC	in HOUSE/SIGN	KARAKA	DIGNITY	GUNA	SEX	MODE	ELEMENT	AIR
1 SELF										
2 VALUES										
3 EFFORT										
4 HOME										
5 CREATE										
6 HEALTH										
7 PARTNER										
8 CHANGE										
9 DHARMA										
10 ACTION										
11 FRIENDS										
12 EXPENSES										
RAHU / KETU										

Date	Time	Location		Name	

ASC

KETU					
VENUS					
SUN					
MOON					
MARS					
RAHU					
JUPITER					
SATURN					
MERCURY					

SUN	MOON	MARS	MERCURY	JUPITER	VENUS	SATURN

— Planet — — Sign —

HOUSE	LORD	RC	in HOUSE/SIGN						KARAKA			DIGNITY	GUNA	SEX	MODE	ELEMENT	AIM
1 SELF																	
2 VALUES																	
3 EFFORT																	
4 HOME																	
5 CREATE																	
6 HEALTH																	
7 PARTNER																	
8 CHANGE																	
9 DHARMA																	
10 ACTION																	
11 FRIENDS																	
12 EXPENSES																	
RAHU / KETU																	

Date	Time	Location	Name

ASC

KETU

VENUS

SUN

MOON

MARS

RAHU

JUPITER

SATURN

MERCURY

SUN	MOON	MARS	MERCURY	JUPITER	VENUS	SATURN

Planet   Sign

HOUSE	LORD	RC	in HOUSE/SIGN	KARAKA	DIGNITY	GUNA	SEX	MODE	ELEMENT	A
1 SELF										
2 VALUES										
3 EFFORT										
4 HOME										
5 CREATE										
6 HEALTH										
7 PARTNER										
8 CHANGE										
9 DHARMA										
10 ACTION										
11 FRIENDS										
12 EXPENSES										
RAHU / KETU										

Date	Time	Location	Name

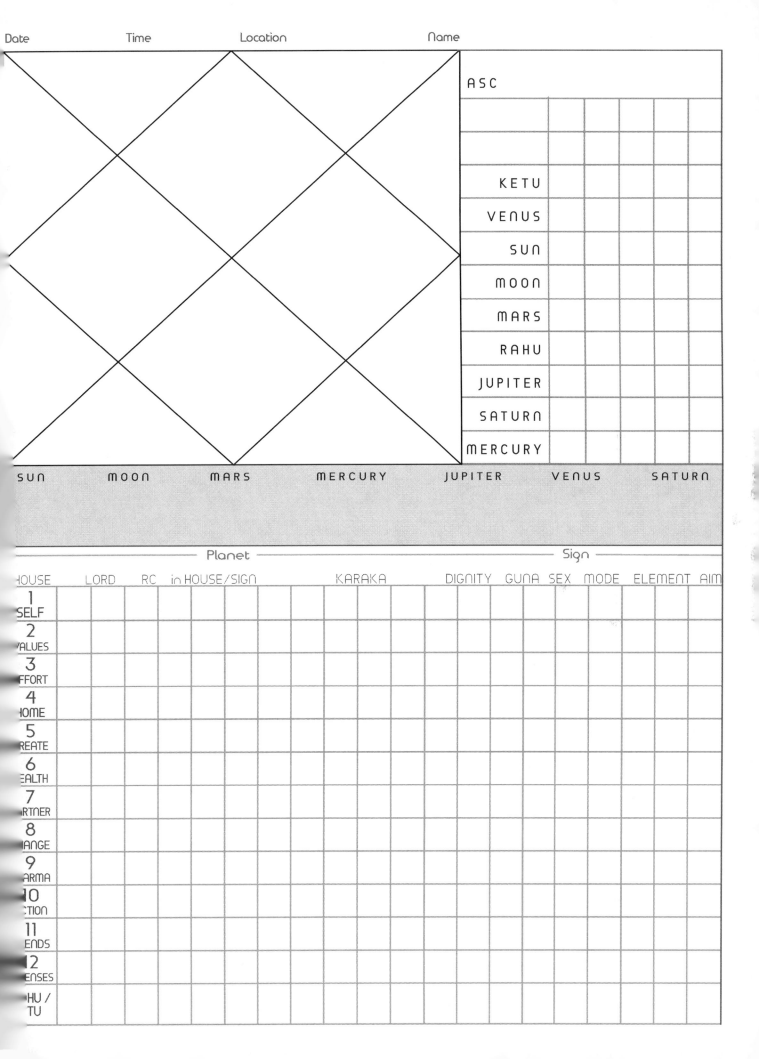

ASC
KETU
VENUS
SUN
MOON
MARS
RAHU
JUPITER
SATURN
MERCURY

SUN	MOON	MARS	MERCURY	JUPITER	VENUS	SATURN

—— Planet ——   —— Sign ——

HOUSE	LORD	RC	in HOUSE/SIGN	KARAKA	DIGNITY	GUNA	SEX	MODE	ELEMENT	AIM
1 SELF										
2 VALUES										
3 EFFORT										
4 HOME										
5 CREATE										
6 HEALTH										
7 PARTNER										
8 CHANGE										
9 DHARMA										
10 ACTION										
11 FRIENDS										
12 EXPENSES										
RAHU / KETU										

Date	Time	Location	Name

ASC

KETU

VENUS

SUN

MOON

MARS

RAHU

JUPITER

SATURN

MERCURY

SUN	MOON	MARS	MERCURY	JUPITER	VENUS	SATURN

	Planet						Sign					
HOUSE	LORD	RC	in HOUSE/SIGN		KARAKA		DIGNITY	GUNA	SEX	MODE	ELEMENT	A
1 SELF												
2 VALUES												
3 EFFORT												
4 HOME												
5 CREATE												
6 HEALTH												
7 PARTNER												
8 CHANGE												
9 DHARMA												
10 ACTION												
11 FRIENDS												
12 EXPENSES												
RAHU / KETU												

Date | Time | Location | Name

ASC

KETU

VENUS

SUN

MOON

MARS

RAHU

JUPITER

SATURN

MERCURY

| SUN | MOON | MARS | MERCURY | JUPITER | VENUS | SATURN |

———— Planet ———————————————————— Sign ————

HOUSE	LORD	RC	in HOUSE/SIGN	KARAKA	DIGNITY	GUNA	SEX	MODE	ELEMENT	AIM
1 SELF										
2 VALUES										
3 EFFORT										
4 HOME										
5 CREATE										
6 HEALTH										
7 PARTNER										
8 CHANGE										
9 DHARMA										
10 ACTION										
11 FRIENDS										
12 SENSES										
RAHU / KETU										

Date	Time	Location	Name

ASC

KETU					
VENUS					
SUN					
MOON					
MARS					
RAHU					
JUPITER					
SATURN					
MERCURY					

SUN	MOON	MARS	MERCURY	JUPITER	VENUS	SATURN

Planet ————————————————— Sign

HOUSE	LORD	RC	in HOUSE/SIGN	KARAKA	DIGNITY	GUNA	SEX	MODE	ELEMENT	A
1 SELF										
2 VALUES										
3 EFFORT										
4 HOME										
5 CREATE										
6 HEALTH										
7 PARTNER										
8 CHANGE										
9 DHARMA										
10 ACTION										
11 FRIENDS										
12 EXPENSES										
RAHU / KETU										

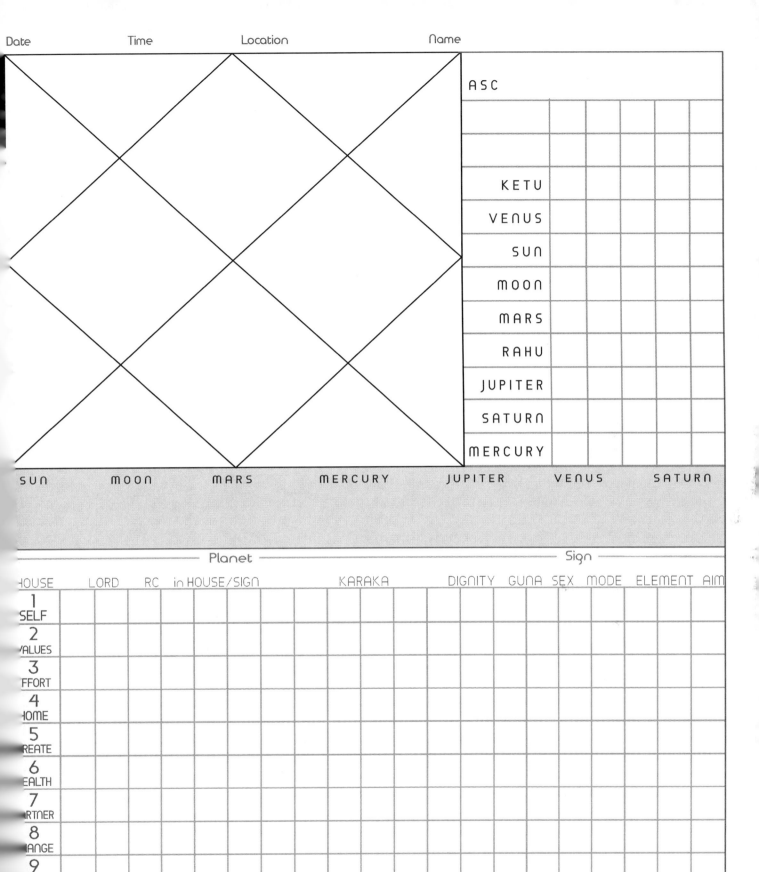

Date   Time   Location   Name

ASC

KETU

VENUS

SUN

MOON

MARS

RAHU

JUPITER

SATURN

MERCURY

SUN	MOON	MARS	MERCURY	JUPITER	VENUS	SATURN

──── Planet ────   ──── Sign ────

HOUSE	LORD	RC	in HOUSE/SIGN	KARAKA	DIGNITY	GUNA	SEX	MODE	ELEMENT	AIM
1 SELF										
2 VALUES										
3 EFFORT										
4 HOME										
5 CREATE										
6 HEALTH										
7 PARTNER										
8 CHANGE										
9 DHARMA										
10 ACTION										
11 FRIENDS										
12 EXPENSES										
RAHU / KETU										

| Date | Time | Location | Name |

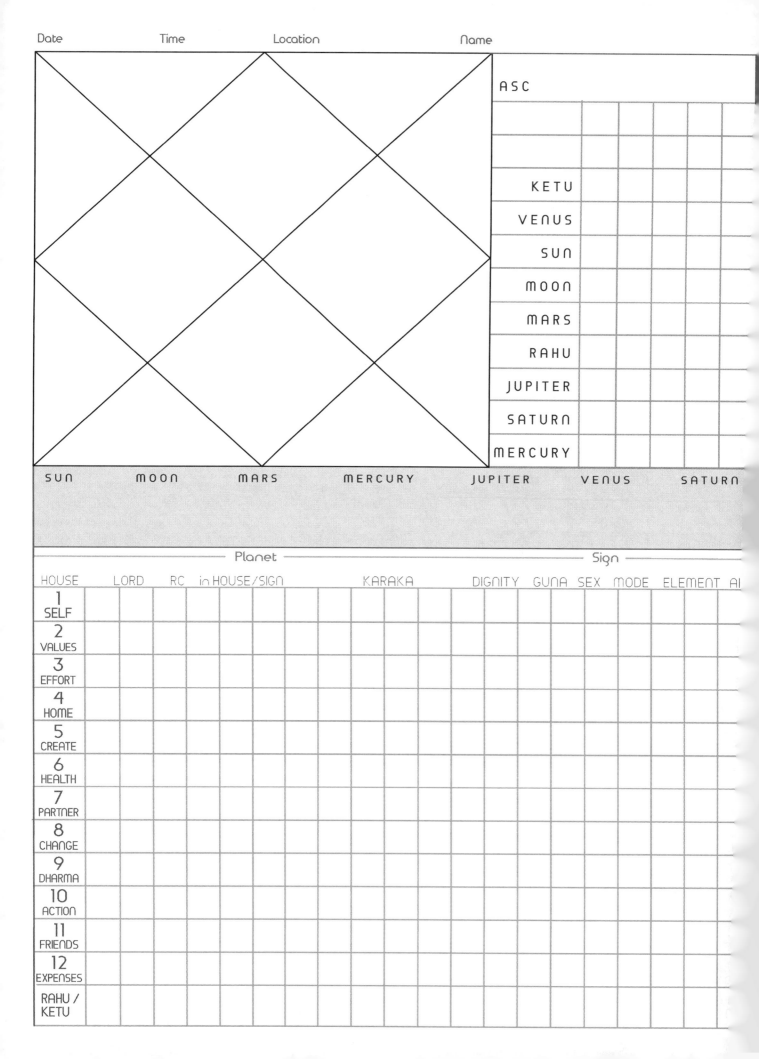

ASC

KETU

VENUS

SUN

MOON

MARS

RAHU

JUPITER

SATURN

MERCURY

| SUN | MOON | MARS | MERCURY | JUPITER | VENUS | SATURN |

	Planet						Sign					
HOUSE	LORD	RC	in HOUSE/SIGN			KARAKA		DIGNITY	GUNA	SEX	MODE	ELEMENT	AI
1 SELF													
2 VALUES													
3 EFFORT													
4 HOME													
5 CREATE													
6 HEALTH													
7 PARTNER													
8 CHANGE													
9 DHARMA													
10 ACTION													
11 FRIENDS													
12 EXPENSES													
RAHU / KETU													

Date	Time	Location	Name

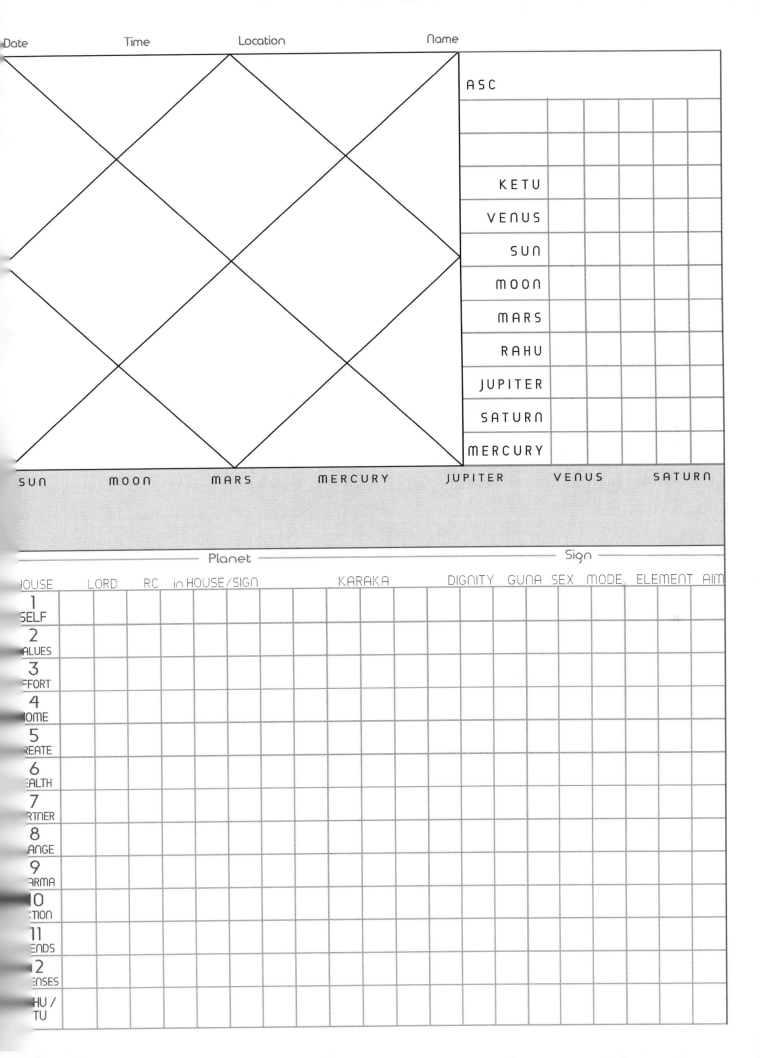

ASC					
KETU					
VENUS					
SUN					
MOON					
MARS					
RAHU					
JUPITER					
SATURN					
MERCURY					

SUN	MOON	MARS	MERCURY	JUPITER	VENUS	SATURN

—— Planet ——   —— Sign ——

HOUSE	LORD	RC	in HOUSE/SIGN	KARAKA	DIGNITY	GUNA	SEX	MODE	ELEMENT	AIM
1 SELF										
2 VALUES										
3 EFFORT										
4 HOME										
5 CREATE										
6 HEALTH										
7 PARTNER										
8 CHANGE										
9 DHARMA										
10 ACTION										
11 FRIENDS										
12 EXPENSES										
RAHU / KETU										

Date   Time   Location   Name

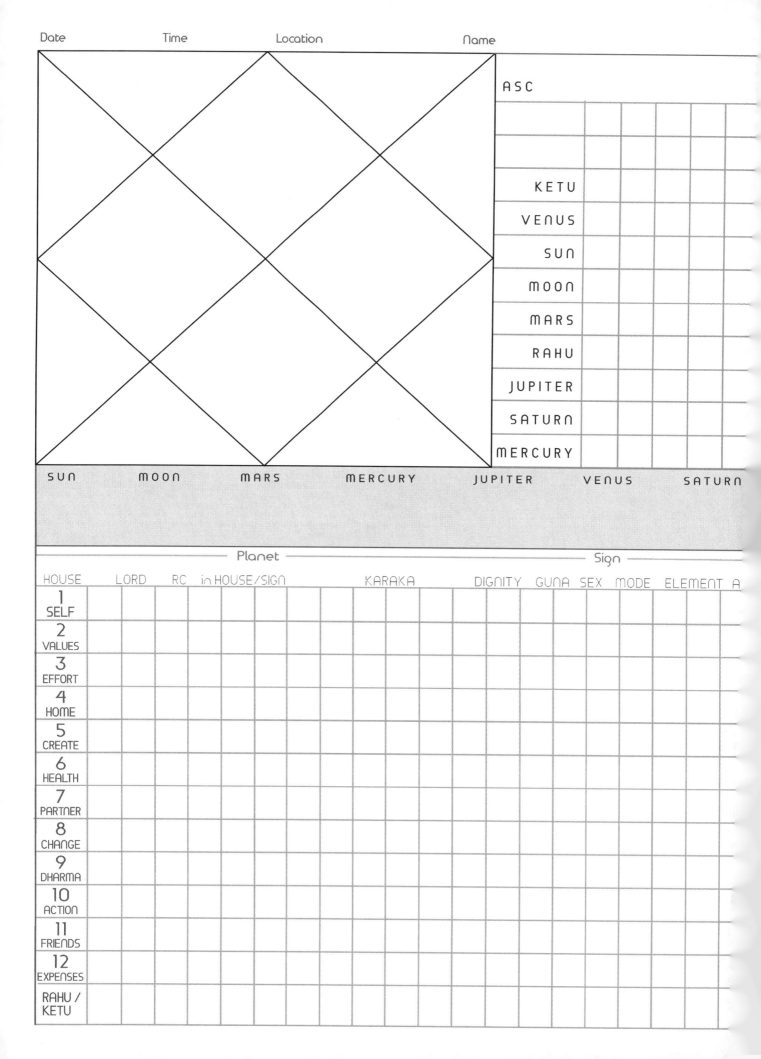

ASC

KETU

VENUS

SUN

MOON

MARS

RAHU

JUPITER

SATURN

MERCURY

SUN   MOON   MARS   MERCURY   JUPITER   VENUS   SATURN

Planet					Sign					
HOUSE	LORD	RC	in HOUSE/SIGN			KARAKA	DIGNITY	GUNA	SEX	MODE	ELEMENT A
1 SELF										
2 VALUES										
3 EFFORT										
4 HOME										
5 CREATE										
6 HEALTH										
7 PARTNER										
8 CHANGE										
9 DHARMA										
10 ACTION										
11 FRIENDS										
12 EXPENSES										
RAHU / KETU										

Date   Time   Location   Name

ASC					
KETU					
VENUS					
SUN					
MOON					
MARS					
RAHU					
JUPITER					
SATURN					
MERCURY					

SUN	MOON	MARS	MERCURY	JUPITER	VENUS	SATURN

———— Planet ————   ———— Sign ————

HOUSE	LORD	RC	in HOUSE/SIGN		KARAKA		DIGNITY	GUNA	SEX	MODE	ELEMENT	AIM
1 SELF												
2 VALUES												
3 EFFORT												
4 HOME												
5 CREATE												
6 HEALTH												
7 PARTNER												
8 CHANGE												
9 DHARMA												
10 ACTION												
11 FRIENDS												
12 EXPENSES												
RAHU / KETU												

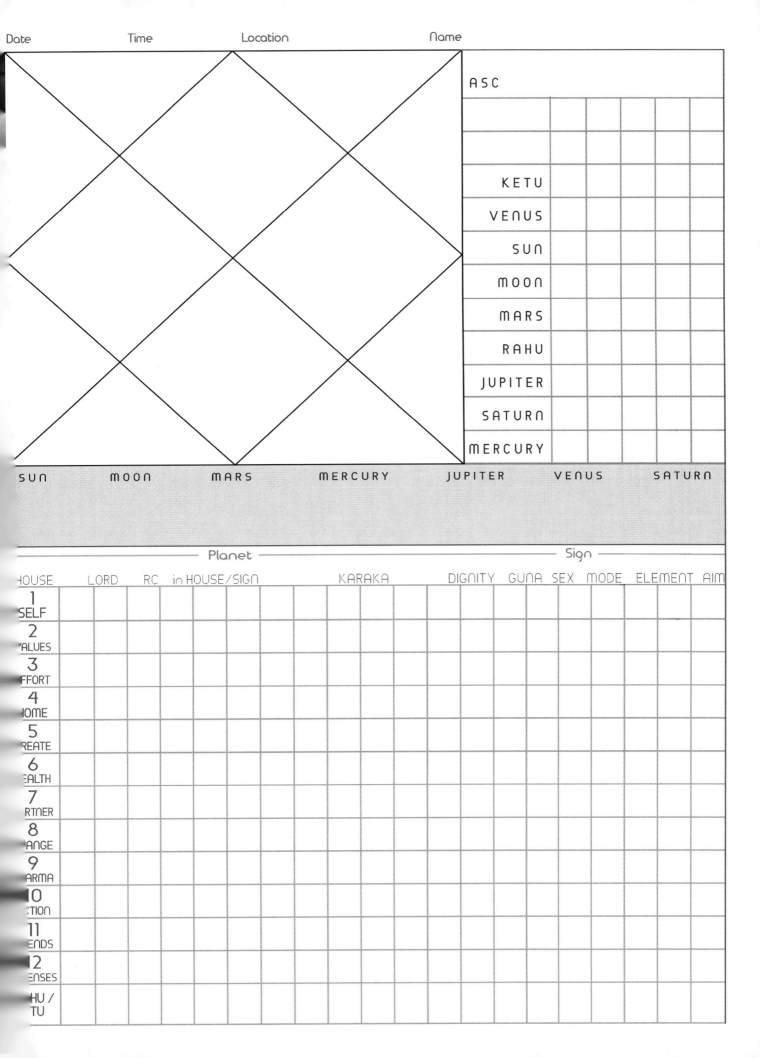

Date   Time   Location   Name

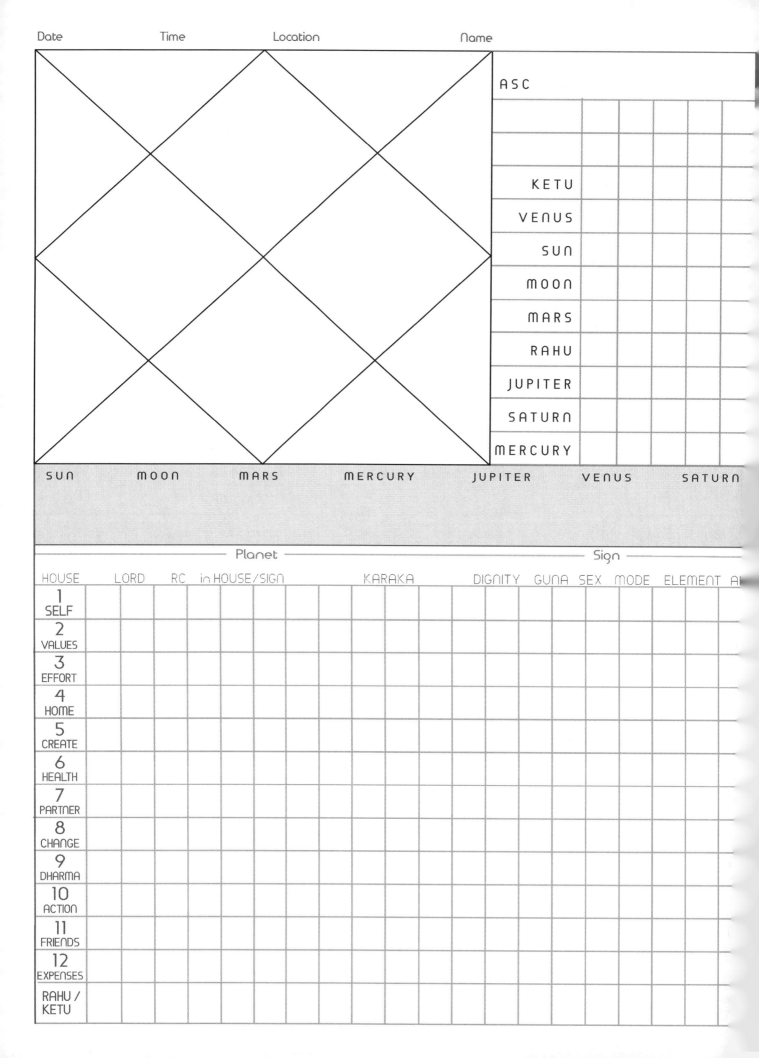

ASC					
KETU					
VENUS					
SUN					
MOON					
MARS					
RAHU					
JUPITER					
SATURN					
MERCURY					

SUN	MOON	MARS	MERCURY	JUPITER	VENUS	SATURN

Planet —————————————— Sign

HOUSE	LORD	RC	in HOUSE/SIGN	KARAKA	DIGNITY	GUNA	SEX	MODE	ELEMENT	A
1 SELF										
2 VALUES										
3 EFFORT										
4 HOME										
5 CREATE										
6 HEALTH										
7 PARTNER										
8 CHANGE										
9 DHARMA										
10 ACTION										
11 FRIENDS										
12 EXPENSES										
RAHU / KETU										

| Date | | Time | | Location | | Name | |

	ASC					

KETU					
VENUS					
SUN					
MOON					
MARS					
RAHU					
JUPITER					
SATURN					
MERCURY					

SUN	MOON	MARS	MERCURY	JUPITER	VENUS	SATURN

— Planet — | — Sign —

HOUSE	LORD	RC	in HOUSE/SIGN	KARAKA	DIGNITY	GUNA	SEX	MODE	ELEMENT	AIM
1 SELF										
2 VALUES										
3 EFFORT										
4 HOME										
5 CREATE										
6 HEALTH										
7 PARTNER										
8 CHANGE										
9 DHARMA										
10 ACTION										
11 FRIENDS										
12 SENSES										
RAHU / KETU										

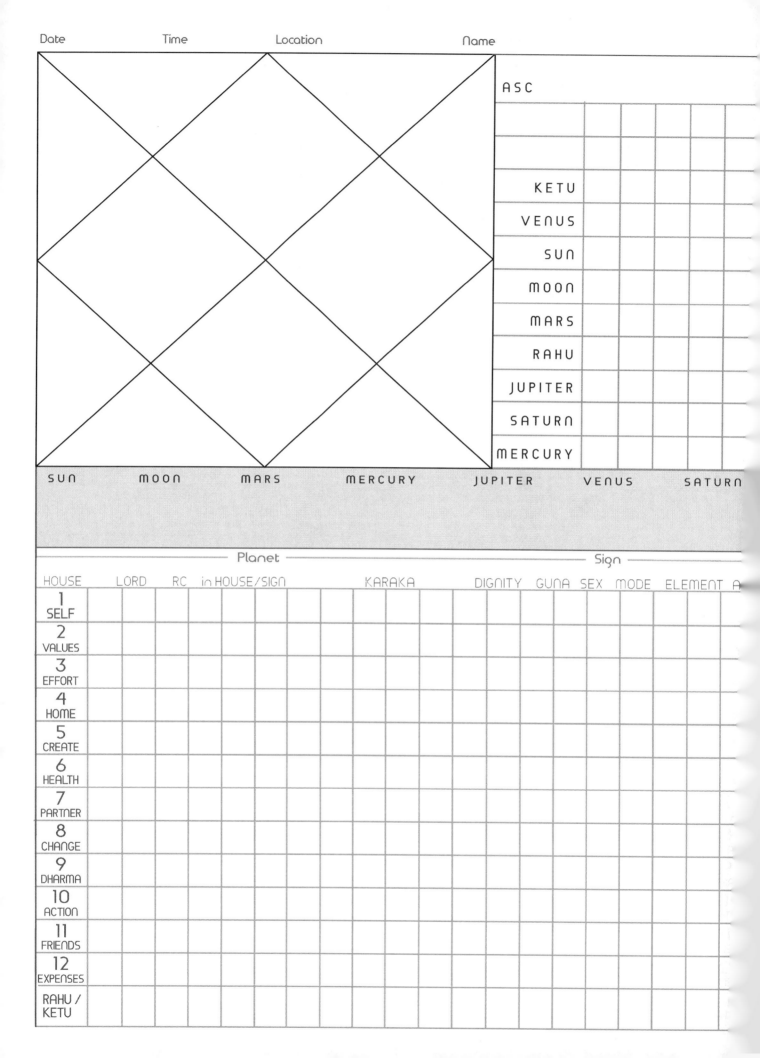

Date   Time   Location   Name

ASC

KETU
VENUS
SUN
MOON
MARS
RAHU
JUPITER
SATURN
MERCURY

SUN   MOON   MARS   MERCURY   JUPITER   VENUS   SATURN

Planet ———————————————————— Sign

HOUSE	LORD	RC	in HOUSE/SIGN	KARAKA	DIGNITY	GUNA	SEX	MODE	ELEMENT	A
1 SELF										
2 VALUES										
3 EFFORT										
4 HOME										
5 CREATE										
6 HEALTH										
7 PARTNER										
8 CHANGE										
9 DHARMA										
10 ACTION										
11 FRIENDS										
12 EXPENSES										
RAHU / KETU										

Date   Time   Location   Name

ASC

KETU				
VENUS				
SUN				
MOON				
MARS				
RAHU				
JUPITER				
SATURN				
MERCURY				

SUN	MOON	MARS	MERCURY	JUPITER	VENUS	SATURN

──────── Planet ────────   ──────── Sign ────────

HOUSE	LORD	RC	in HOUSE/SIGN	KARAKA	DIGNITY	GUNA	SEX	MODE	ELEMENT	AIM
1 SELF										
2 VALUES										
3 EFFORT										
4 HOME										
5 CREATE										
6 HEALTH										
7 PARTNER										
8 CHANGE										
9 DHARMA										
10 ACTION										
11 FRIENDS										
12 SENSES										
RAHU / KETU										

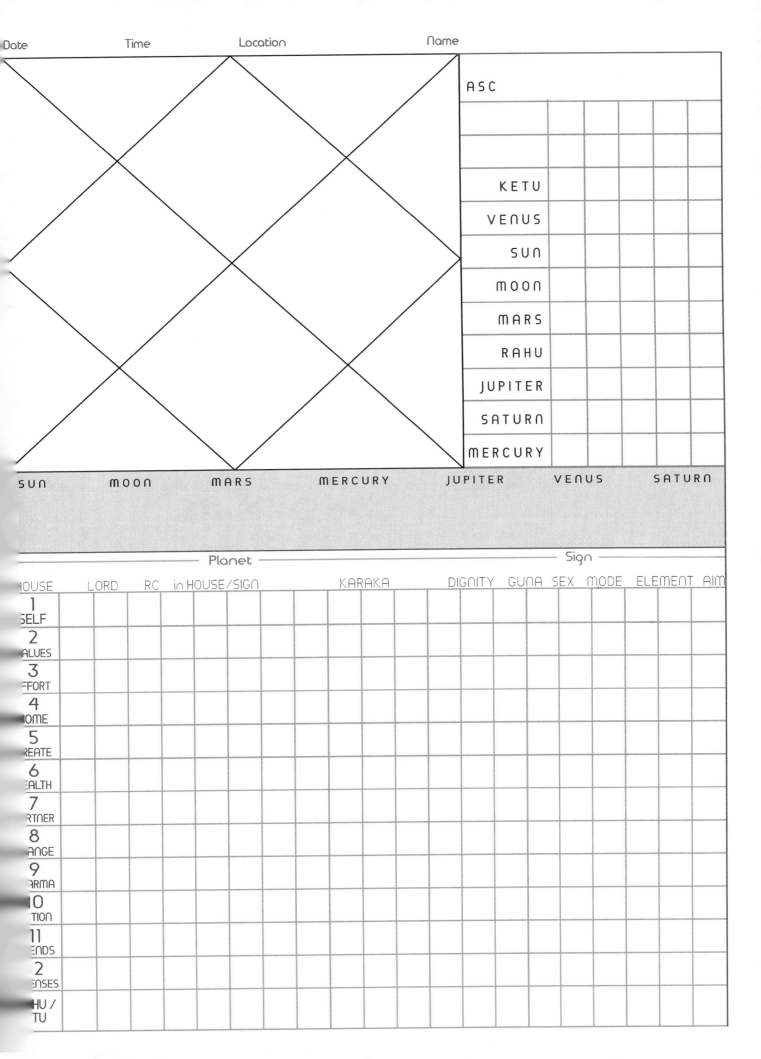

Date   Time   Location   Name

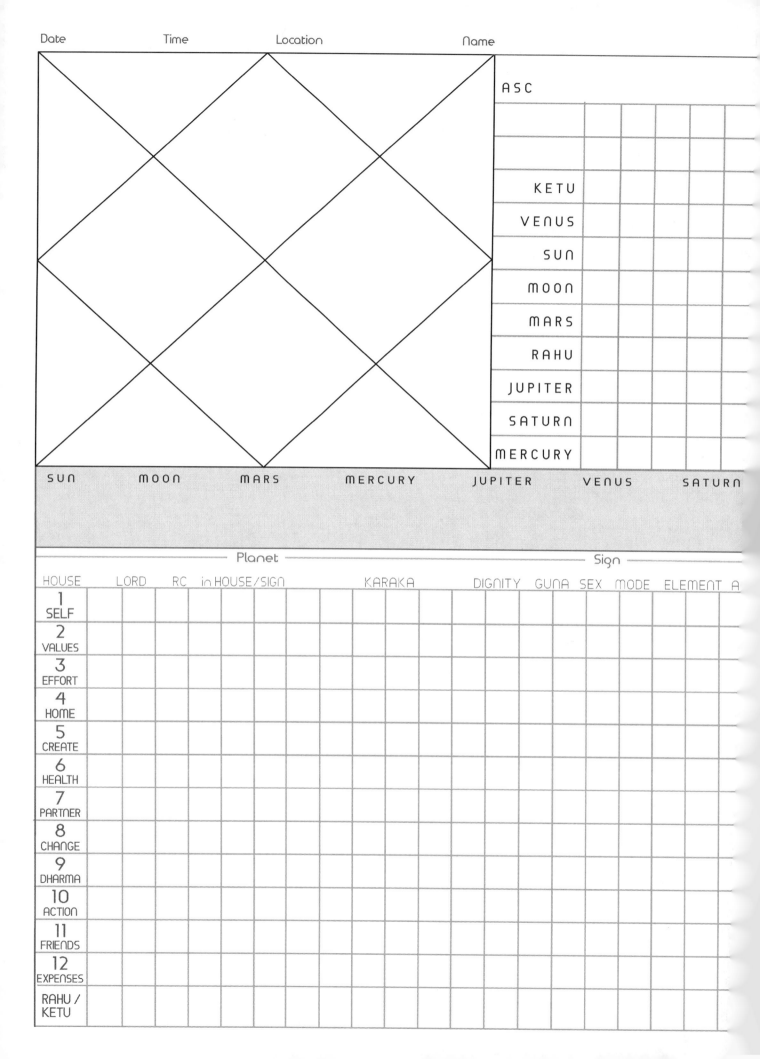

ASC

	KETU		
VENUS		
SUN		
MOON		
MARS		
RAHU		
JUPITER		
SATURN		
MERCURY		

| SUN | MOON | MARS | MERCURY | JUPITER | VENUS | SATURN |

Planet —————————————————— Sign

HOUSE	LORD	RC	in HOUSE/SIGN	KARAKA	DIGNITY	GUNA	SEX	MODE	ELEMENT	A
1 SELF										
2 VALUES										
3 EFFORT										
4 HOME										
5 CREATE										
6 HEALTH										
7 PARTNER										
8 CHANGE										
9 DHARMA										
10 ACTION										
11 FRIENDS										
12 EXPENSES										
RAHU / KETU										

Date | Time | Location | Name

ASC

KETU

VENUS

SUN

MOON

MARS

RAHU

JUPITER

SATURN

MERCURY

| SUN | MOON | MARS | MERCURY | JUPITER | VENUS | SATURN |

Planet ─── Sign

HOUSE	LORD	RC	in HOUSE/SIGN	KARAKA	DIGNITY	GUNA	SEX	MODE	ELEMENT	AIM
1 SELF										
2 VALUES										
3 EFFORT										
4 HOME										
5 CREATE										
6 HEALTH										
7 PARTNER										
8 CHANGE										
9 DHARMA										
10 ACTION										
11 FRIENDS										
12 EXPENSES										
RAHU / KETU										

Date   Time   Location   Name

ASC

KETU	
VENUS	
SUN	
MOON	
MARS	
RAHU	
JUPITER	
SATURN	
MERCURY	

SUN   MOON   MARS   MERCURY   JUPITER   VENUS   SATURN

Planet   Sign

HOUSE	LORD	RC	in HOUSE/SIGN	KARAKA	DIGNITY	GUNA	SEX	MODE	ELEMENT	A
1 SELF										
2 VALUES										
3 EFFORT										
4 HOME										
5 CREATE										
6 HEALTH										
7 PARTNER										
8 CHANGE										
9 DHARMA										
10 ACTION										
11 FRIENDS										
12 EXPENSES										
RAHU / KETU										

Date	Time	Location	Name

ASC

KETU					
VENUS					
SUN					
MOON					
MARS					
RAHU					
JUPITER					
SATURN					
MERCURY					

SUN	MOON	MARS	MERCURY	JUPITER	VENUS	SATURN

──── Planet ────					──── Sign ────						
HOUSE	LORD	RC	in HOUSE/SIGN	KARAKA	DIGNITY	GUNA	SEX	MODE	ELEMENT	AIM
1 SELF										
2 VALUES										
3 EFFORT										
4 HOME										
5 CREATE										
6 HEALTH										
7 PARTNER										
8 CHANGE										
9 DHARMA										
10 ACTION										
11 FRIENDS										
12 SENSES										
RAHU / KETU										

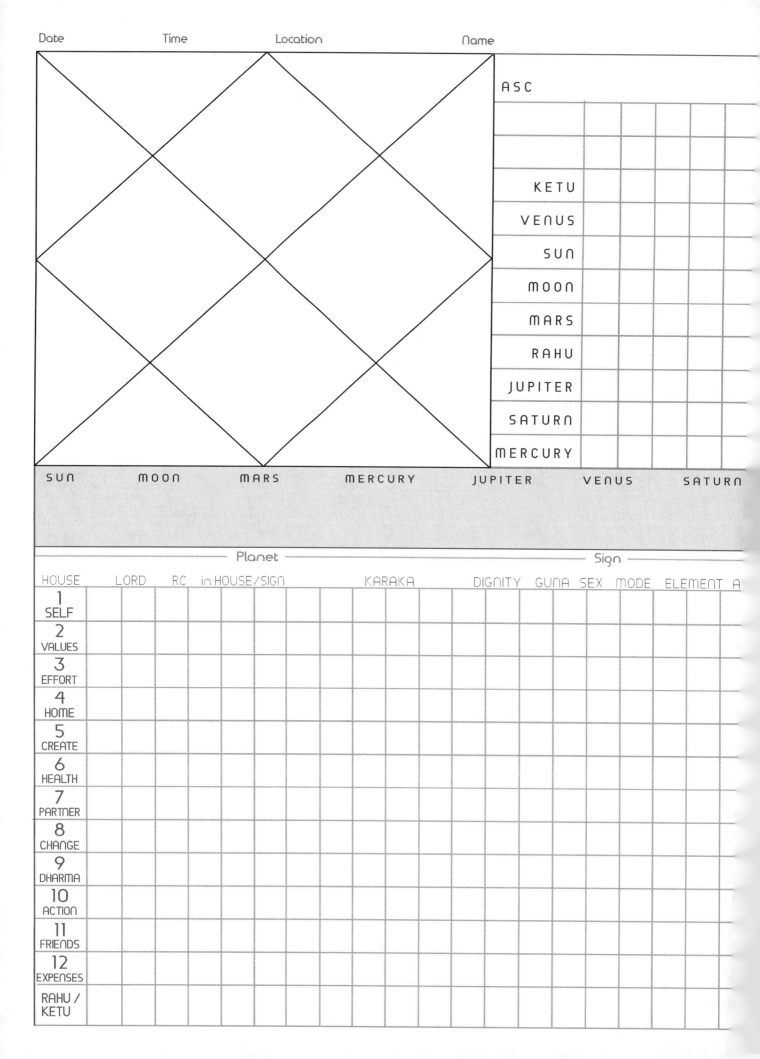

Date   Time   Location   Name

ASC

KETU
VENUS
SUN
MOON
MARS
RAHU
JUPITER
SATURN
MERCURY

| SUN | MOON | MARS | MERCURY | JUPITER | VENUS | SATURN |

Planet ———————————————————————————— Sign

HOUSE	LORD	RC	in HOUSE/SIGN	KARAKA	DIGNITY	GUNA	SEX	MODE	ELEMENT	A
1 SELF										
2 VALUES										
3 EFFORT										
4 HOME										
5 CREATE										
6 HEALTH										
7 PARTNER										
8 CHANGE										
9 DHARMA										
10 ACTION										
11 FRIENDS										
12 EXPENSES										
RAHU / KETU										

Date	Time	Location	Name

				ASC					
				KETU					
				VENUS					
				SUN					
				MOON					
				MARS					
				RAHU					
				JUPITER					
				SATURN					
				MERCURY					

SUN	MOON	MARS	MERCURY	JUPITER	VENUS	SATURN

──── Planet ────   ──── Sign ────

HOUSE	LORD	RC	in HOUSE/SIGN		KARAKA	DIGNITY	GUNA	SEX	MODE	ELEMENT	AIM
1 SELF											
2 VALUES											
3 EFFORT											
4 HOME											
5 CREATE											
6 HEALTH											
7 PARTNER											
8 CHANGE											
9 DHARMA											
10 ACTION											
11 FRIENDS											
12 SENSES											
RAHU / KETU											

Date   Time   Location   Name

ASC

KETU

VENUS

SUN

MOON

MARS

RAHU

JUPITER

SATURN

MERCURY

SUN	MOON	MARS	MERCURY	JUPITER	VENUS	SATURN

Planet ——————————————————————————————— Sign

HOUSE	LORD	RC	in HOUSE/SIGN			KARAKA		DIGNITY	GUNA	SEX	MODE	ELEMENT	A
1 SELF													
2 VALUES													
3 EFFORT													
4 HOME													
5 CREATE													
6 HEALTH													
7 PARTNER													
8 CHANGE													
9 DHARMA													
10 ACTION													
11 FRIENDS													
12 EXPENSES													
RAHU / KETU													

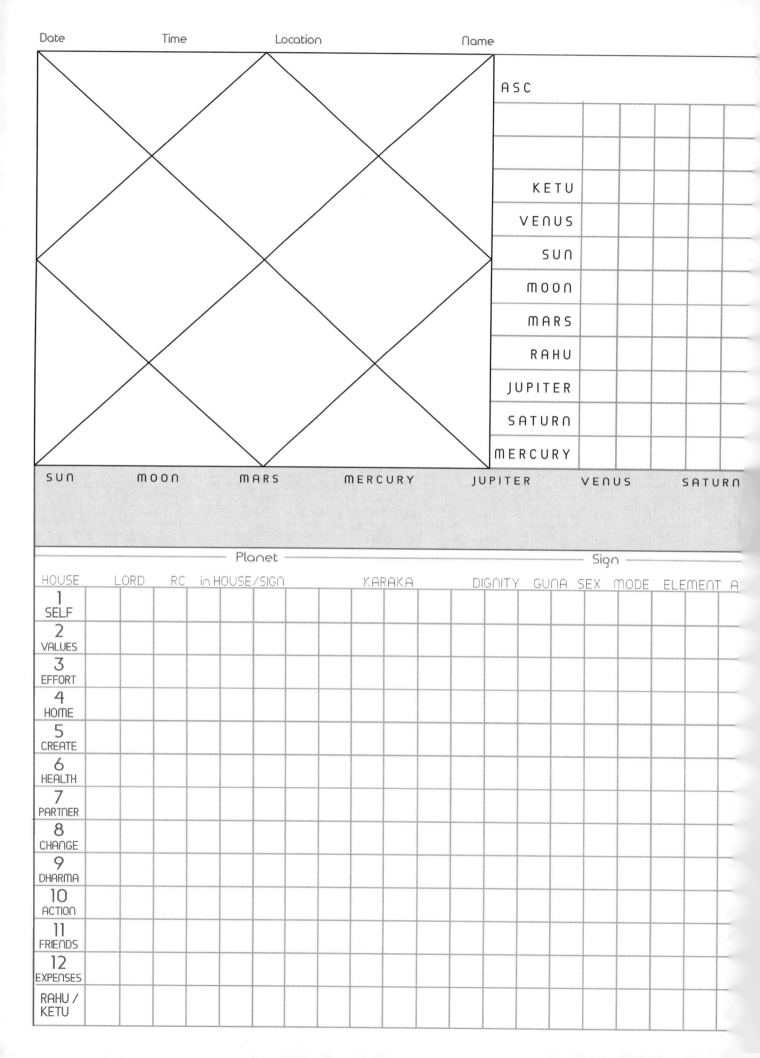

Date   Time   Location   Name

ASC					
KETU					
VENUS					
SUN					
MOON					
MARS					
RAHU					
JUPITER					
SATURN					
MERCURY					

SUN	MOON	MARS	MERCURY	JUPITER	VENUS	SATURN

— Planet —   — Sign —

HOUSE	LORD	RC	in HOUSE/SIGN			KARAKA			DIGNITY	GUNA	SEX	MODE	ELEMENT	AIM
1 SELF														
2 VALUES														
3 EFFORT														
4 HOME														
5 CREATE														
6 HEALTH														
7 PARTNER														
8 CHANGE														
9 DHARMA														
10 ACTION														
11 FRIENDS														
12 SENSES														
RAHU / KETU														

ASC

KETU

VENUS

SUN

MOON

MARS

RAHU

JUPITER

SATURN

MERCURY

| SUN | MOON | MARS | MERCURY | JUPITER | VENUS | SATURN |

Planet —————————————————————————————— Sign

HOUSE	LORD	RC	in HOUSE/SIGN	KARAKA	DIGNITY	GUNA	SEX	MODE	ELEMENT	A
1 SELF										
2 VALUES										
3 EFFORT										
4 HOME										
5 CREATE										
6 HEALTH										
7 PARTNER										
8 CHANGE										
9 DHARMA										
10 ACTION										
11 FRIENDS										
12 EXPENSES										
RAHU / KETU										

Date	Time	Location	Name

ASC					
KETU					
VENUS					
SUN					
MOON					
MARS					
RAHU					
JUPITER					
SATURN					
MERCURY					

SUN	MOON	MARS	MERCURY	JUPITER	VENUS	SATURN

	Planet					Sign					
HOUSE	LORD	RC	in HOUSE/SIGN	KARAKA		DIGNITY	GUNA	SEX	MODE	ELEMENT	AIM
1 SELF											
2 VALUES											
3 EFFORT											
4 HOME											
5 CREATE											
6 HEALTH											
7 PARTNER											
8 CHANGE											
9 DHARMA											
10 ACTION											
11 FRIENDS											
12 SENSES											
RAHU / KETU											

| Date | Time | Location | Name |

ASC

| KETU |
| VENUS |
| SUN |
| MOON |
| MARS |
| RAHU |
| JUPITER |
| SATURN |
| MERCURY |

| SUN | MOON | MARS | MERCURY | JUPITER | VENUS | SATURN |

Planet								Sign				
HOUSE	LORD	RC	in HOUSE/SIGN		KARAKA		DIGNITY	GUNA	SEX	MODE	ELEMENT	A
1 SELF												
2 VALUES												
3 EFFORT												
4 HOME												
5 CREATE												
6 HEALTH												
7 PARTNER												
8 CHANGE												
9 DHARMA												
10 ACTION												
11 FRIENDS												
12 EXPENSES												
RAHU / KETU												

Date	Time	Location	Name

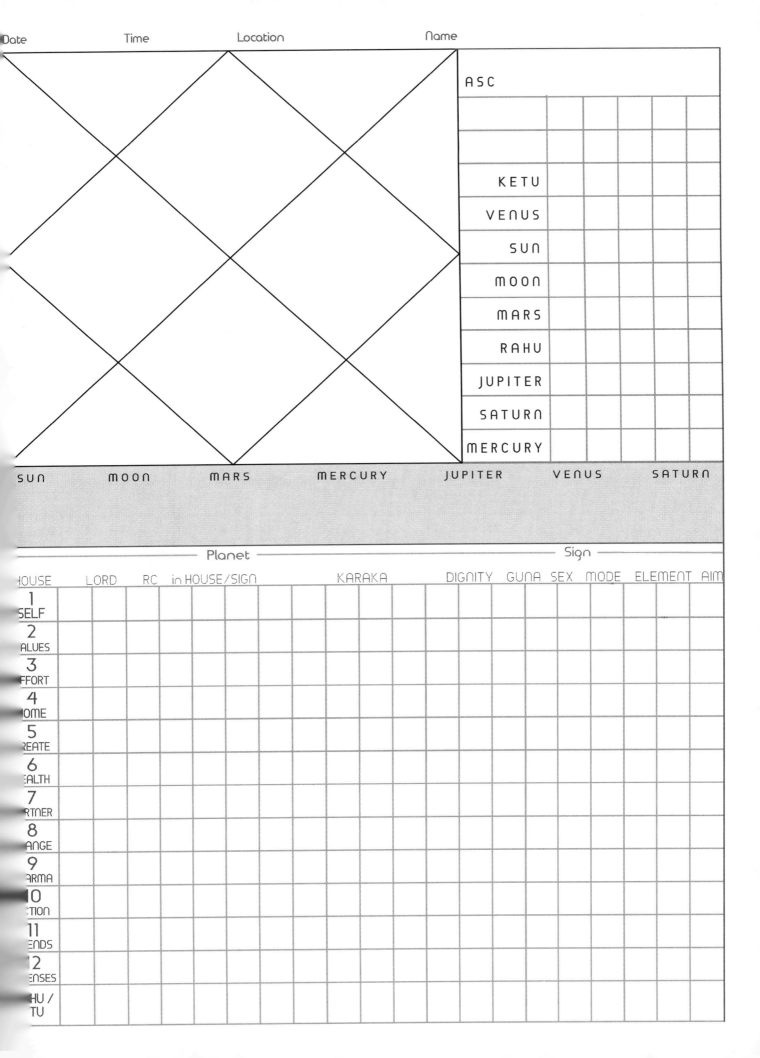

ASC

| KETU |
| VENUS |
| SUN |
| MOON |
| MARS |
| RAHU |
| JUPITER |
| SATURN |
| MERCURY |

SUN	MOON	MARS	MERCURY	JUPITER	VENUS	SATURN

		Planet						Sign					
HOUSE	LORD	RC	in HOUSE/SIGN			KARAKA		DIGNITY	GUNA	SEX	MODE	ELEMENT	AIM
1 SELF													
2 VALUES													
3 EFFORT													
4 HOME													
5 CREATE													
6 HEALTH													
7 PARTNER													
8 CHANGE													
9 DHARMA													
10 ACTION													
11 FRIENDS													
12 EXPENSES													
RAHU / KETU													

Date   Time   Location   Name

ASC

KETU

VENUS

SUN

MOON

MARS

RAHU

JUPITER

SATURN

MERCURY

SUN	MOON	MARS	MERCURY	JUPITER	VENUS	SATURN

Planet   Sign

HOUSE	LORD	RC	in HOUSE/SIGN	KARAKA	DIGNITY	GUNA	SEX	MODE	ELEMENT	A
1 SELF										
2 VALUES										
3 EFFORT										
4 HOME										
5 CREATE										
6 HEALTH										
7 PARTNER										
8 CHANGE										
9 DHARMA										
10 ACTION										
11 FRIENDS										
12 EXPENSES										
RAHU / KETU										

Date	Time	Location	Name

ASC

| KETU |
| VENUS |
| SUN |
| MOON |
| MARS |
| RAHU |
| JUPITER |
| SATURN |
| MERCURY |

SUN	MOON	MARS	MERCURY	JUPITER	VENUS	SATURN

	Planet						Sign					
HOUSE	LORD	RC	in HOUSE/SIGN		KARAKA		DIGNITY	GUNA	SEX	MODE	ELEMENT	AIM
1 SELF												
2 VALUES												
3 EFFORT												
4 HOME												
5 CREATE												
6 HEALTH												
7 PARTNER												
8 CHANGE												
9 DHARMA												
10 ACTION												
11 FRIENDS												
12 SENSES												
RAHU / KETU												

Date　　　　Time　　　　Location　　　　Name

ASC

KETU

VENUS

SUN

MOON

MARS

RAHU

JUPITER

SATURN

MERCURY

| SUN | MOON | MARS | MERCURY | JUPITER | VENUS | SATURN |

Planet　　　　　　　　　　　　　　　　　Sign

HOUSE	LORD	RC	in HOUSE/SIGN			KARAKA	DIGNITY	GUNA	SEX	MODE	ELEMENT	A
1 SELF												
2 VALUES												
3 EFFORT												
4 HOME												
5 CREATE												
6 HEALTH												
7 PARTNER												
8 CHANGE												
9 DHARMA												
10 ACTION												
11 FRIENDS												
12 EXPENSES												
RAHU / KETU												

Date   Time   Location   Name

ASC

KETU					
VENUS					
SUN					
MOON					
MARS					
RAHU					
JUPITER					
SATURN					
MERCURY					

SUN	MOON	MARS	MERCURY	JUPITER	VENUS	SATURN

―――――――――― Planet ―――――――――― ―――――― Sign ――――――

HOUSE	LORD	RC	in HOUSE/SIGN			KARAKA		DIGNITY	GUNA	SEX	MODE	ELEMENT	AIM
1 SELF													
2 VALUES													
3 EFFORT													
4 HOME													
5 CREATE													
6 HEALTH													
7 PARTNER													
8 CHANGE													
9 DHARMA													
10 ACTION													
11 FRIENDS													
12 SENSES													
RAHU / KETU													

Date Time Location Name

ASC

KETU
VENUS
SUN
MOON
MARS
RAHU
JUPITER
SATURN
MERCURY

| SUN | MOON | MARS | MERCURY | JUPITER | VENUS | SATURN |

Planet ———————————— Sign

HOUSE	LORD	RC	in HOUSE/SIGN				KARAKA		DIGNITY	GUNA	SEX	MODE	ELEMENT	A
1 SELF														
2 VALUES														
3 EFFORT														
4 HOME														
5 CREATE														
6 HEALTH														
7 PARTNER														
8 CHANGE														
9 DHARMA														
10 ACTION														
11 FRIENDS														
12 EXPENSES														
RAHU / KETU														

Date	Time	Location	Name

ASC					
KETU					
VENUS					
SUN					
MOON					
MARS					
RAHU					
JUPITER					
SATURN					
MERCURY					

SUN	MOON	MARS	MERCURY	JUPITER	VENUS	SATURN

—— Planet ——   —— Sign ——

HOUSE	LORD	RC	in HOUSE/SIGN	KARAKA	DIGNITY	GUNA	SEX	MODE	ELEMENT	AIM
1 SELF										
2 VALUES										
3 EFFORT										
4 HOME										
5 CREATE										
6 HEALTH										
7 PARTNER										
8 CHANGE										
9 DHARMA										
10 ACTION										
11 FRIENDS										
12 SENSES										
RAHU / KETU										

Date	Time	Location	Name

ASC

KETU				
VENUS				
SUN				
MOON				
MARS				
RAHU				
JUPITER				
SATURN				
MERCURY				

SUN	MOON	MARS	MERCURY	JUPITER	VENUS	SATURN

Planet ————————————————————————— Sign

HOUSE	LORD	RC	in HOUSE/SIGN	KARAKA	DIGNITY	GUNA	SEX	MODE	ELEMENT	A
1 SELF										
2 VALUES										
3 EFFORT										
4 HOME										
5 CREATE										
6 HEALTH										
7 PARTNER										
8 CHANGE										
9 DHARMA										
10 ACTION										
11 FRIENDS										
12 EXPENSES										
RAHU / KETU										

Date   Time   Location   Name

ASC					
KETU					
VENUS					
SUN					
MOON					
MARS					
RAHU					
JUPITER					
SATURN					
MERCURY					

SUN	MOON	MARS	MERCURY	JUPITER	VENUS	SATURN

Planet ─── Sign

HOUSE	LORD	RC	in HOUSE/SIGN			KARAKA			DIGNITY	GUNA	SEX	MODE	ELEMENT	AIM
1 SELF														
2 VALUES														
3 EFFORT														
4 HOME														
5 CREATE														
6 HEALTH														
7 PARTNER														
8 CHANGE														
9 DHARMA														
10 ACTION														
11 FRIENDS														
12 EXPENSES														
RAHU / KETU														

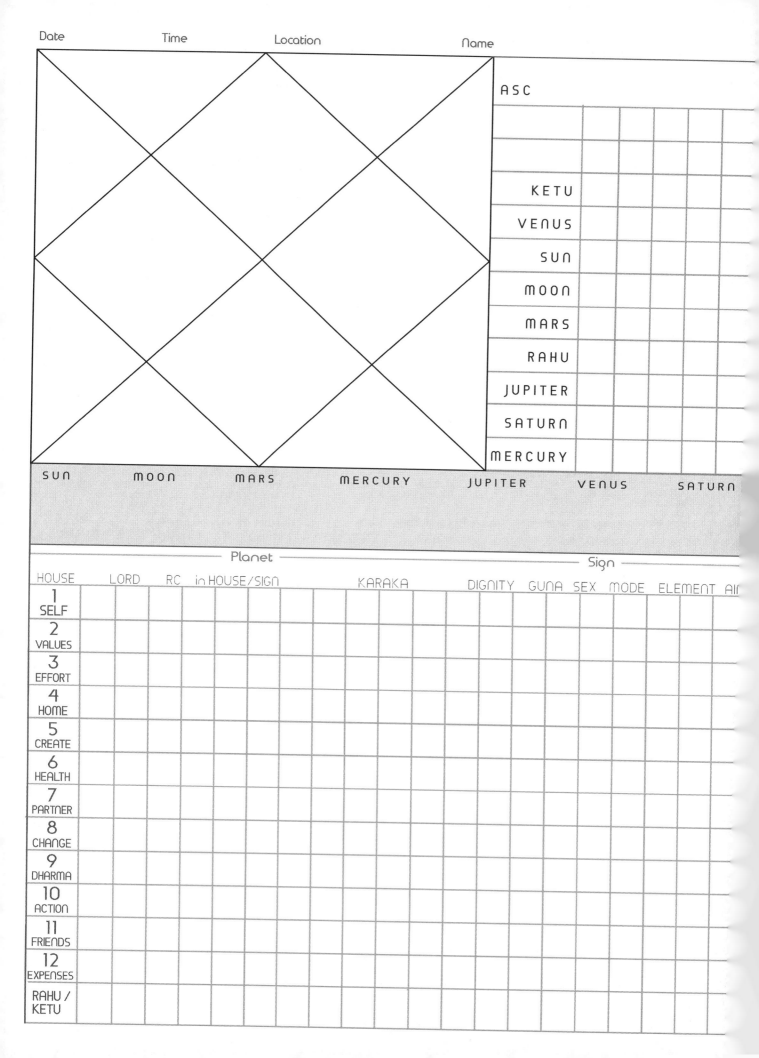

Date	Time	Location	Name

ASC

KETU

VENUS

SUN

MOON

MARS

RAHU

JUPITER

SATURN

MERCURY

SUN	MOON	MARS	MERCURY	JUPITER	VENUS	SATURN

Planet — Sign

HOUSE	LORD	RC	in HOUSE/SIGN	KARAKA	DIGNITY	GUNA	SEX	MODE	ELEMENT	AIR
1 SELF										
2 VALUES										
3 EFFORT										
4 HOME										
5 CREATE										
6 HEALTH										
7 PARTNER										
8 CHANGE										
9 DHARMA										
10 ACTION										
11 FRIENDS										
12 EXPENSES										
RAHU / KETU										

| Date | Time | Location | Name |

ASC

KETU				
VENUS				
SUN				
MOON				
MARS				
RAHU				
JUPITER				
SATURN				
MERCURY				

| SUN | MOON | MARS | MERCURY | JUPITER | VENUS | SATURN |

Planet — **Sign**

HOUSE	LORD	RC	in HOUSE/SIGN	KARAKA	DIGNITY	GUNA	SEX	MODE	ELEMENT	AIM
1 SELF										
2 VALUES										
3 EFFORT										
4 HOME										
5 CREATE										
6 HEALTH										
7 PARTNER										
8 CHANGE										
9 DHARMA										
10 ACTION										
11 FRIENDS										
12 SENSES										
RAHU / KETU										

Date	Time	Location	Name

ASC

| KETU |
| VENUS |
| SUN |
| MOON |
| MARS |
| RAHU |
| JUPITER |
| SATURN |
| MERCURY |

SUN	MOON	MARS	MERCURY	JUPITER	VENUS	SATURN

Planet ——————————————————————————————————— Sign

HOUSE	LORD	RC	in HOUSE/SIGN	KARAKA	DIGNITY	GUNA	SEX	MODE	ELEMENT	A
1 SELF										
2 VALUES										
3 EFFORT										
4 HOME										
5 CREATE										
6 HEALTH										
7 PARTNER										
8 CHANGE										
9 DHARMA										
10 ACTION										
11 FRIENDS										
12 EXPENSES										
RAHU / KETU										

Date   Time   Location   Name

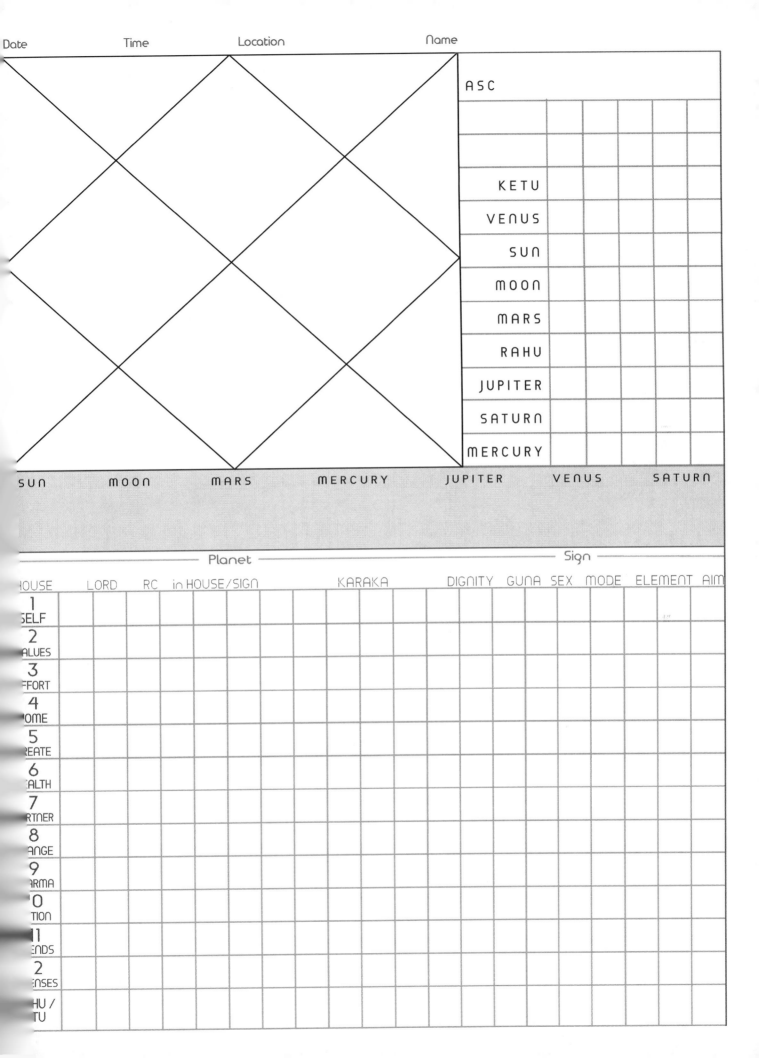

ASC

KETU					
VENUS					
SUN					
MOON					
MARS					
RAHU					
JUPITER					
SATURN					
MERCURY					

SUN   MOON   MARS   MERCURY   JUPITER   VENUS   SATURN

—— Planet ——   —— Sign ——

HOUSE	LORD	RC	in HOUSE/SIGN	KARAKA	DIGNITY	GUNA	SEX	MODE	ELEMENT	AIM
1 SELF										
2 VALUES										
3 EFFORT										
4 HOME										
5 CREATE										
6 HEALTH										
7 PARTNER										
8 CHANGE										
9 DHARMA										
10 ACTION										
11 FRIENDS										
12 EXPENSES										
RAHU / KETU										

Date   Time   Location   Name

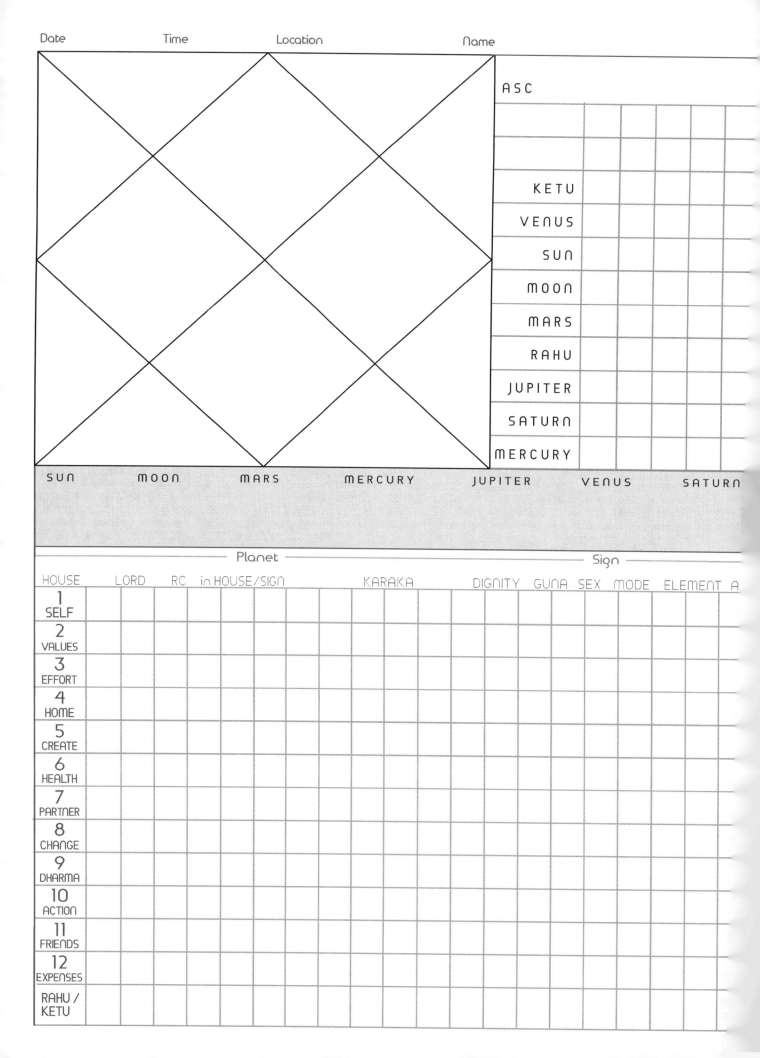

ASC

KETU					
VENUS					
SUN					
MOON					
MARS					
RAHU					
JUPITER					
SATURN					
MERCURY					

SUN	MOON	MARS	MERCURY	JUPITER	VENUS	SATURN

Planet ————— Sign

HOUSE	LORD	RC	in HOUSE/SIGN	KARAKA	DIGNITY	GUNA	SEX	MODE	ELEMENT	A
1 SELF										
2 VALUES										
3 EFFORT										
4 HOME										
5 CREATE										
6 HEALTH										
7 PARTNER										
8 CHANGE										
9 DHARMA										
10 ACTION										
11 FRIENDS										
12 EXPENSES										
RAHU / KETU										

Date	Time	Location	Name

ASC

KETU					
VENUS					
SUN					
MOON					
MARS					
RAHU					
JUPITER					
SATURN					
MERCURY					

SUN	MOON	MARS	MERCURY	JUPITER	VENUS	SATURN

———— Planet ————   ———— Sign ————

HOUSE	LORD	RC	in HOUSE/SIGN	KARAKA	DIGNITY	GUNA	SEX	MODE	ELEMENT	AIM
1 SELF										
2 VALUES										
3 EFFORT										
4 HOME										
5 CREATE										
6 HEALTH										
7 PARTNER										
8 CHANGE										
9 DHARMA										
10 ACTION										
11 FRIENDS										
12 SENSES										
RAHU / KETU										

Date	Time	Location	Name

ASC

KETU

VENUS

SUN

MOON

MARS

RAHU

JUPITER

SATURN

MERCURY

SUN	MOON	MARS	MERCURY	JUPITER	VENUS	SATURN

Planet — Sign

HOUSE	LORD	RC	in HOUSE/SIGN	KARAKA	DIGNITY	GUNA	SEX	MODE	ELEMENT	F
1 SELF										
2 VALUES										
3 EFFORT										
4 HOME										
5 CREATE										
6 HEALTH										
7 PARTNER										
8 CHANGE										
9 DHARMA										
10 ACTION										
11 FRIENDS										
12 EXPENSES										
RAHU / KETU										

Date   Time   Location   Name

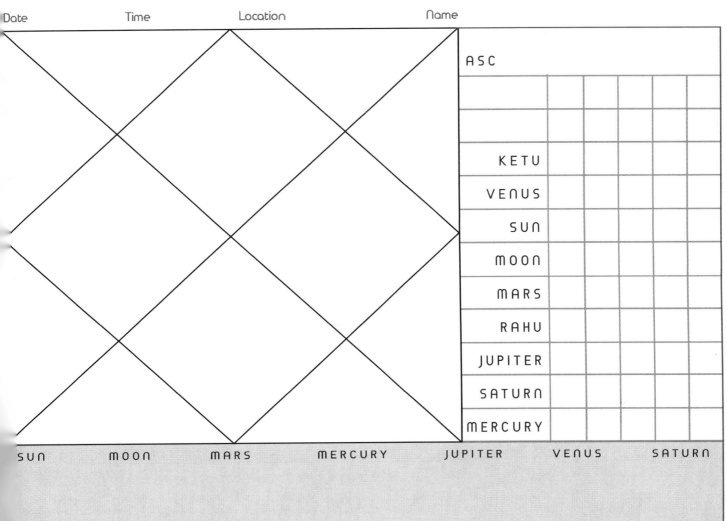

ASC					
KETU					
VENUS					
SUN					
MOON					
MARS					
RAHU					
JUPITER					
SATURN					
MERCURY					

SUN	MOON	MARS	MERCURY	JUPITER	VENUS	SATURN

——— Planet ———   ——— Sign ———

HOUSE	LORD	RC	in HOUSE/SIGN	KARAKA	DIGNITY	GUNA	SEX	MODE	ELEMENT	AIM
1 SELF										
2 VALUES										
3 EFFORT										
4 HOME										
5 CREATE										
6 HEALTH										
7 PARTNER										
8 CHANGE										
9 DHARMA										
10 ACTION										
11 FRIENDS										
12 SENSES										
RAHU / KETU										

Date	Time	Location	Name

ASC

KETU					
VENUS					
SUN					
MOON					
MARS					
RAHU					
JUPITER					
SATURN					
MERCURY					

SUN	MOON	MARS	MERCURY	JUPITER	VENUS	SATURN

Planet ———————————————————————— Sign

HOUSE	LORD	RC	in HOUSE/SIGN	KARAKA	DIGNITY	GUNA	SEX	MODE	ELEMENT	A
1 SELF										
2 VALUES										
3 EFFORT										
4 HOME										
5 CREATE										
6 HEALTH										
7 PARTNER										
8 CHANGE										
9 DHARMA										
10 ACTION										
11 FRIENDS										
12 EXPENSES										
RAHU / KETU										

| Date | Time | Location | Name |

ASC

KETU
VENUS
SUN
MOON
MARS
RAHU
JUPITER
SATURN
MERCURY

| SUN | MOON | MARS | MERCURY | JUPITER | VENUS | SATURN |

---------- Planet ---------- ---------- Sign ----------

HOUSE	LORD	RC	in HOUSE/SIGN	KARAKA	DIGNITY	GUNA	SEX	MODE	ELEMENT	AIM
1 SELF										
2 VALUES										
3 EFFORT										
4 HOME										
5 CREATE										
6 HEALTH										
7 PARTNER										
8 CHANGE										
9 DHARMA										
10 ACTION										
11 FRIENDS										
12 SENSES										
RAHU / KETU										

Date	Time	Location	Name

ASC

KETU

VENUS

SUN

MOON

MARS

RAHU

JUPITER

SATURN

MERCURY

SUN	MOON	MARS	MERCURY	JUPITER	VENUS	SATUR

	Planet							Sign				
HOUSE	LORD	RC	in HOUSE/SIGN		KARAKA		DIGNITY	GUNA	SEX	MODE	ELEMENT
1 SELF											
2 VALUES											
3 EFFORT											
4 HOME											
5 CREATE											
6 HEALTH											
7 PARTNER											
8 CHANGE											
9 DHARMA											
10 ACTION											
11 FRIENDS											
12 EXPENSES											
RAHU / KETU											

Date Time Location Name

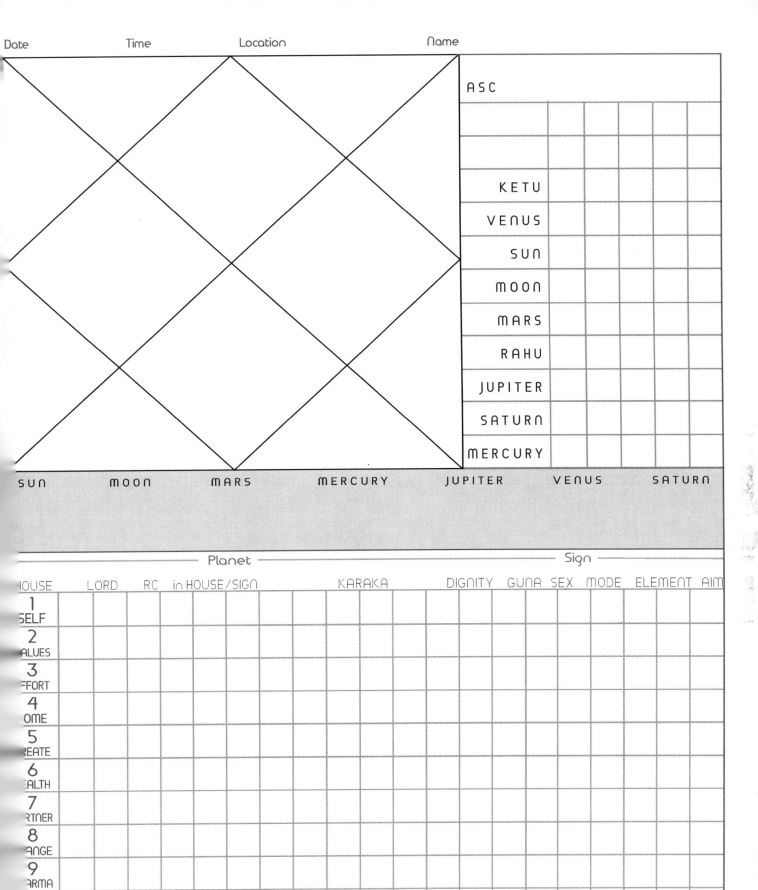

ASC

| KETU |
| VENUS |
| SUN |
| MOON |
| MARS |
| RAHU |
| JUPITER |
| SATURN |
| MERCURY |

| SUN | MOON | MARS | MERCURY | JUPITER | VENUS | SATURN |

——————— Planet ——————— ——————— Sign ———————

HOUSE	LORD	RC	in HOUSE/SIGN	KARAKA	DIGNITY	GUNA	SEX	MODE	ELEMENT	AIM
1 SELF										
2 VALUES										
3 EFFORT										
4 HOME										
5 CREATE										
6 HEALTH										
7 PARTNER										
8 CHANGE										
9 DHARMA										
10 ACTION										
11 FRIENDS										
12 SENSES										
RAHU / KETU										

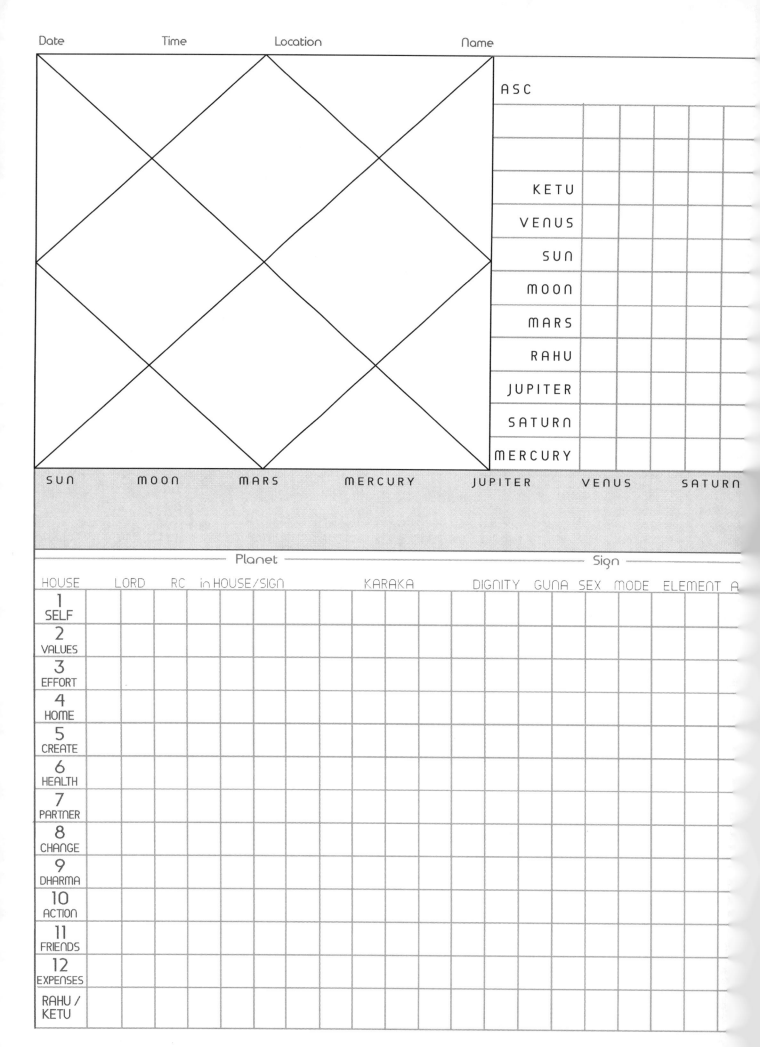

Date Time Location Name

ASC

KETU
VENUS
SUN
MOON
MARS
RAHU
JUPITER
SATURN
MERCURY

| SUN | MOON | MARS | MERCURY | JUPITER | VENUS | SATURN |

Planet — Sign

HOUSE	LORD	RC	in HOUSE/SIGN	KARAKA	DIGNITY	GUNA	SEX	MODE	ELEMENT	A
1 SELF										
2 VALUES										
3 EFFORT										
4 HOME										
5 CREATE										
6 HEALTH										
7 PARTNER										
8 CHANGE										
9 DHARMA										
10 ACTION										
11 FRIENDS										
12 EXPENSES										
RAHU / KETU										

Date   Time   Location   Name

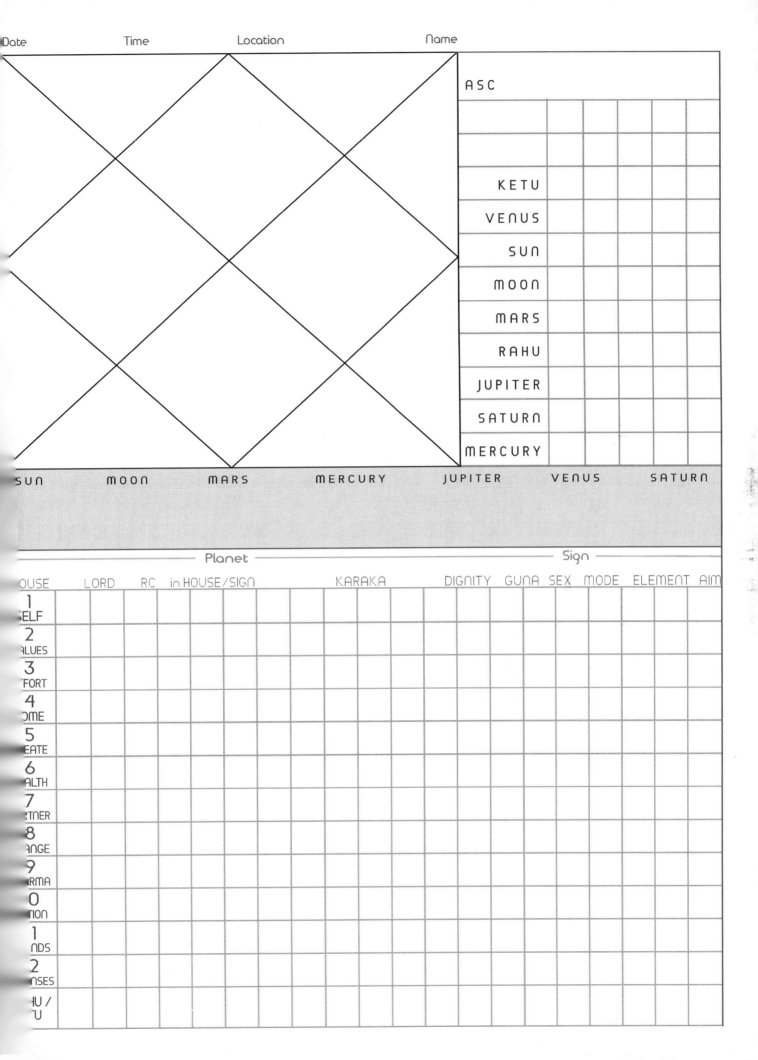

ASC

KETU					
VENUS					
SUN					
MOON					
MARS					
RAHU					
JUPITER					
SATURN					
MERCURY					

SUN	MOON	MARS	MERCURY	JUPITER	VENUS	SATURN

——— Planet ———   ——— Sign ———

HOUSE	LORD	RC	in HOUSE/SIGN	KARAKA	DIGNITY	GUNA	SEX	MODE	ELEMENT	AIM
1 SELF										
2 VALUES										
3 EFFORT										
4 HOME										
5 CREATE										
6 HEALTH										
7 PARTNER										
8 CHANGE										
9 DHARMA										
10 ACTION										
11 FRIENDS										
12 SENSES										
RAHU / KETU										

Date	Time	Location	Name

ASC

KETU					
VENUS					
SUN					
MOON					
MARS					
RAHU					
JUPITER					
SATURN					
MERCURY					

SUN	MOON	MARS	MERCURY	JUPITER	VENUS	SATURN

Planet ———————————————————— Sign

HOUSE	LORD	RC	in HOUSE/SIGN		KARAKA		DIGNITY	GUNA	SEX	MODE	ELEMENT	
1 SELF												
2 VALUES												
3 EFFORT												
4 HOME												
5 CREATE												
6 HEALTH												
7 PARTNER												
8 CHANGE												
9 DHARMA												
10 ACTION												
11 FRIENDS												
12 EXPENSES												
RAHU / KETU												

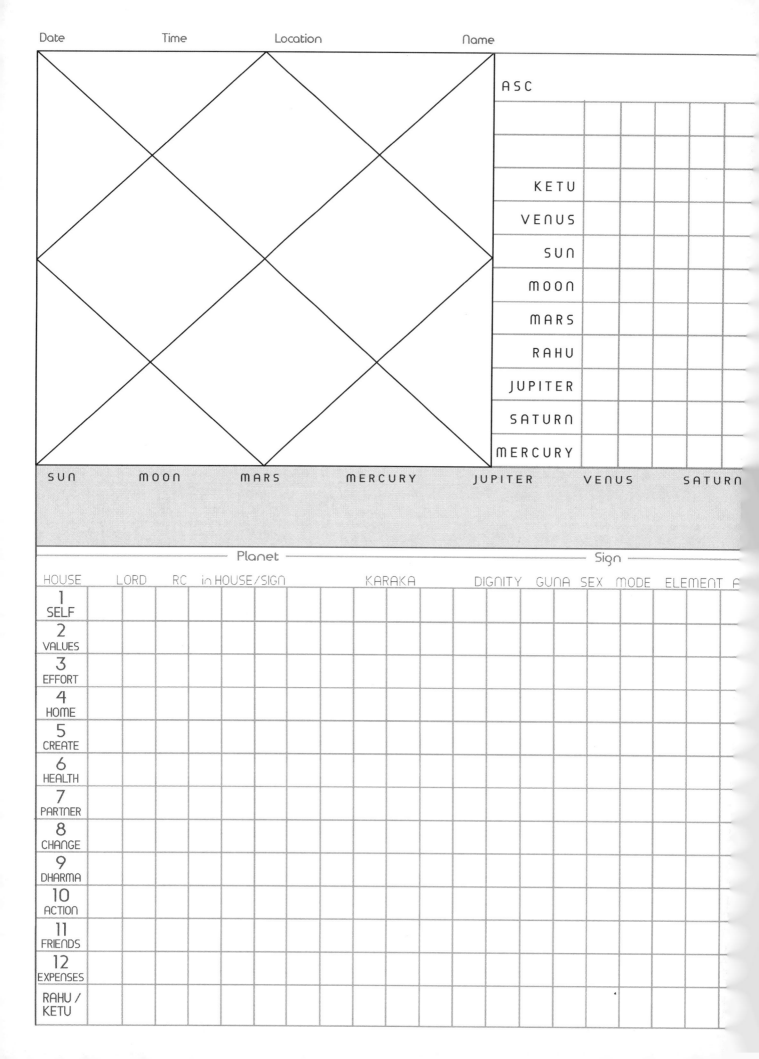

Date	Time	Location	Name

ASC

KETU					
VENUS					
SUN					
MOON					
MARS					
RAHU					
JUPITER					
SATURN					
MERCURY					

SUN	MOON	MARS	MERCURY	JUPITER	VENUS	SATURN

	Planet					Sign					
HOUSE	LORD	RC	in HOUSE/SIGN	KARAKA	DIGNITY	GUNA	SEX	MODE	ELEMENT	AIM
1 SELF										
2 VALUES										
3 EFFORT										
4 HOME										
5 CREATE										
6 HEALTH										
7 PARTNER										
8 CHANGE										
9 DHARMA										
10 ACTION										
11 FRIENDS										
12 SENSES										
RAHU / KETU										

Date	Time	Location	Name

ASC

KETU

VENUS

SUN

MOON

MARS

RAHU

JUPITER

SATURN

MERCURY

SUN	MOON	MARS	MERCURY	JUPITER	VENUS	SATURN

Planet ———————————————————————————————— Sign

HOUSE	LORD	RC	in HOUSE/SIGN	KARAKA	DIGNITY	GUNA	SEX	MODE	ELEMENT	
1 SELF										
2 VALUES										
3 EFFORT										
4 HOME										
5 CREATE										
6 HEALTH										
7 PARTNER										
8 CHANGE										
9 DHARMA										
10 ACTION										
11 FRIENDS										
12 EXPENSES										
RAHU / KETU										

ASC					
KETU					
VENUS					
SUN					
MOON					
MARS					
RAHU					
JUPITER					
SATURN					
MERCURY					

SUN　　　MOON　　　MARS　　　MERCURY　　　JUPITER　　　VENUS　　　SATURN

Planet ———— Sign

HOUSE	LORD	RC	in HOUSE/SIGN			KARAKA		DIGNITY	GUNA	SEX	MODE	ELEMENT	AIM
1 SELF													
2 VALUES													
3 EFFORT													
4 HOME													
5 CREATE													
6 HEALTH													
7 PARTNER													
8 CHANGE													
9 DHARMA													
10 ACTION													
11 FRIENDS													
12 SENSES													
RAHU / KETU													

Date   Time   Location   Name

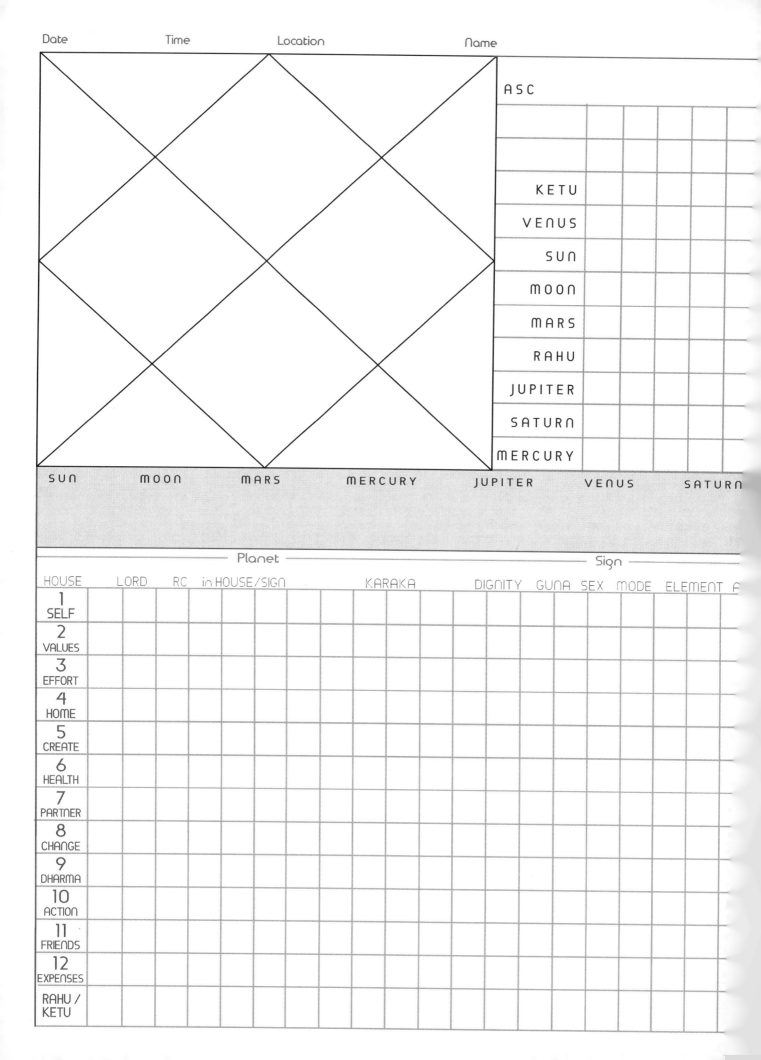

ASC

KETU

VENUS

SUN

MOON

MARS

RAHU

JUPITER

SATURN

MERCURY

SUN   MOON   MARS   MERCURY   JUPITER   VENUS   SATURN

Planet ———————————————————————— Sign

HOUSE	LORD	RC	in HOUSE/SIGN	KARAKA	DIGNITY	GUNA	SEX	MODE	ELEMENT	F
1 SELF										
2 VALUES										
3 EFFORT										
4 HOME										
5 CREATE										
6 HEALTH										
7 PARTNER										
8 CHANGE										
9 DHARMA										
10 ACTION										
11 FRIENDS										
12 EXPENSES										
RAHU / KETU										

Time   Location   Name

ASC

| KETU |
| VENUS |
| SUN |
| MOON |
| MARS |
| RAHU |
| JUPITER |
| SATURN |
| MERCURY |

N	MOON	MARS	MERCURY	JUPITER	VENUS	SATURN

—————— Planet ——————   —————— Sign ——————

SE	LORD	RC	in HOUSE/SIGN	KARAKA	DIGNITY	GUNA	SEX	MODE	ELEMENT	AIM
F										
ES										
RT										
IE										
TE										
TH										
IER										
IGE										
MA										
ON										
IDS										
ISES										
U/ U										

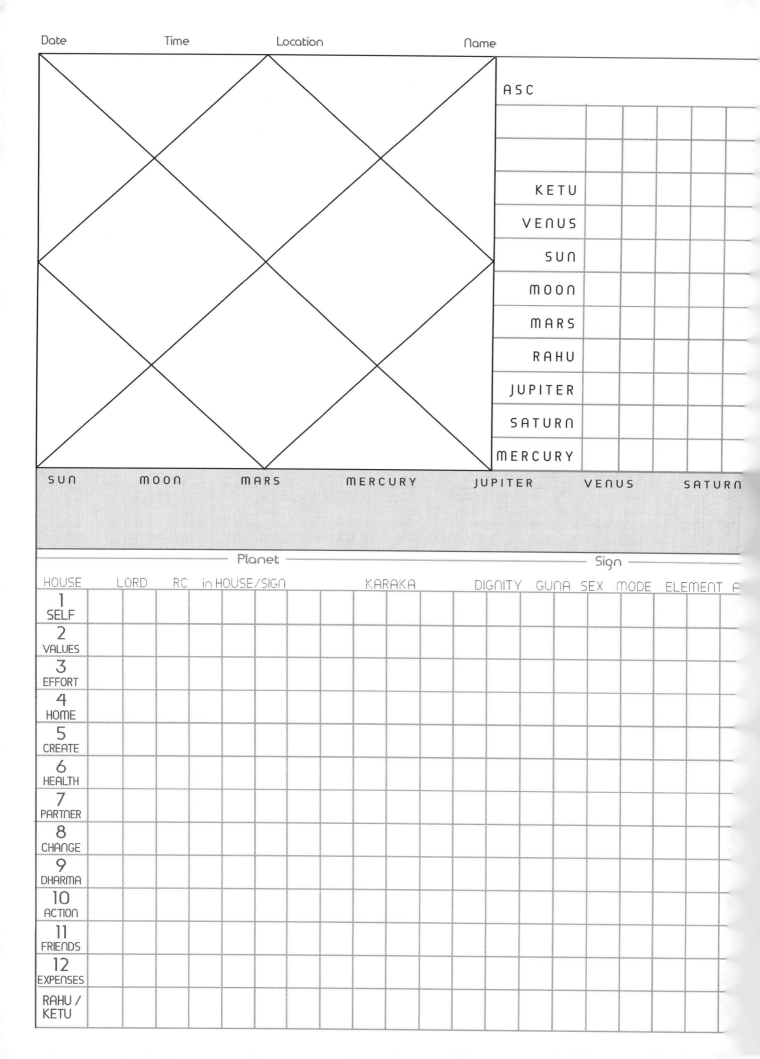

ASC

KETU

VENUS

SUN

MOON

MARS

RAHU

JUPITER

SATURN

MERCURY

| SUN | MOON | MARS | MERCURY | JUPITER | VENUS | SATURN |

Planet —————————————————————— Sign

HOUSE	LORD	RC	in HOUSE/SIGN	KARAKA	DIGNITY	GUNA	SEX	MODE	ELEMENT	
1 SELF										
2 VALUES										
3 EFFORT										
4 HOME										
5 CREATE										
6 HEALTH										
7 PARTNER										
8 CHANGE										
9 DHARMA										
10 ACTION										
11 FRIENDS										
12 EXPENSES										
RAHU / KETU										

ASC					
KETU					
VENUS					
SUN					
MOON					
MARS					
RAHU					
JUPITER					
SATURN					
MERCURY					

SUN	MOON	MARS	MERCURY	JUPITER	VENUS	SATURN

	Planet					Sign					
HOUSE	LORD	RC	in HOUSE/SIGN			KARAKA	DIGNITY	GUNA	SEX	MODE	ELEMENT	AIM
1 SELF												
2 VALUES												
3 EFFORT												
4 HOME												
5 CREATE												
6 HEALTH												
7 PARTNER												
8 CHANGE												
9 DHARMA												
10 ACTION												
11 FRIENDS												
12 SENSES												
RAHU / KETU												

Date	Time	Location	Name

ASC

| KETU |
| VENUS |
| SUN |
| MOON |
| MARS |
| RAHU |
| JUPITER |
| SATURN |
| MERCURY |

SUN	MOON	MARS	MERCURY	JUPITER	VENUS	SATURN

Planet ——————————————————————————— Sign

HOUSE	LORD	RC	in HOUSE/SIGN	KARAKA	DIGNITY	GUNA	SEX	MODE	ELEMENT	F
1 SELF										
2 VALUES										
3 EFFORT										
4 HOME										
5 CREATE										
6 HEALTH										
7 PARTNER										
8 CHANGE										
9 DHARMA										
10 ACTION										
11 FRIENDS										
12 EXPENSES										
RAHU / KETU										

ASC

| KETU |
| VENUS |
| SUN |
| MOON |
| MARS |
| RAHU |
| JUPITER |
| SATURN |
| MERCURY |

SUN   MOON   MARS   MERCURY   JUPITER   VENUS   SATURN

Planet ——————————————————————— Sign ———

HOUSE	LORD	RC	in HOUSE/SIGN	KARAKA	DIGNITY	GUNA	SEX	MODE	ELEMENT	AIM
1 SELF										
2 VALUES										
3 EFFORT										
4 HOME										
5 CREATE										
6 HEALTH										
7 PARTNER										
8 CHANGE										
9 DHARMA										
10 ACTION										
11 FRIENDS										
12 SENSES										
RAHU / KETU										

Date	Time	Location	Name

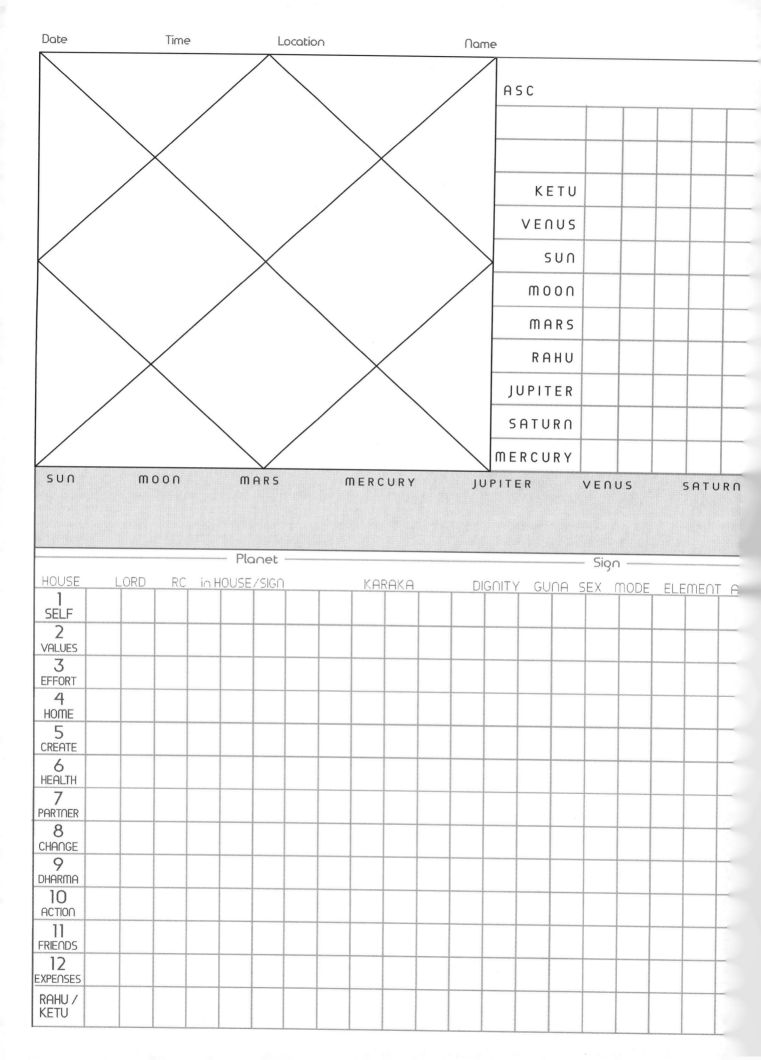

ASC

KETU

VENUS

SUN

MOON

MARS

RAHU

JUPITER

SATURN

MERCURY

SUN	MOON	MARS	MERCURY	JUPITER	VENUS	SATURN

Planet ——— Sign

HOUSE	LORD	RC	in HOUSE/SIGN	KARAKA	DIGNITY	GUNA	SEX	MODE	ELEMENT	A
1 SELF										
2 VALUES										
3 EFFORT										
4 HOME										
5 CREATE										
6 HEALTH										
7 PARTNER										
8 CHANGE										
9 DHARMA										
10 ACTION										
11 FRIENDS										
12 EXPENSES										
RAHU / KETU										

Made in the USA
Las Vegas, NV
22 October 2024

10279425R00068